PIRI PIRI MAB
of the Kupai Omasker Working Party

The Journey to Legal Recognition of the
Torres Strait Islander Child Rearing Practice

Compiled by Paul Ban

First published 2022 by Paul Ban

Produced by Independent Ink
independentink.com.au

Back cover image: The Working Party, Brisbane, October 2022.

Cover design by Maria Biaggini
Edited by Sabine Borgis
Internal design by Independent Ink
Typeset in 12/17 pt Adobe Garamond Pro by Post Pre-press Group, Brisbane

A catalogue record for this book is available from the National Library of Australia

ISBN 978-0-6456644-0-9 (paperback)
ISBN 978-0-6456644-1-6 (epub)

Contents

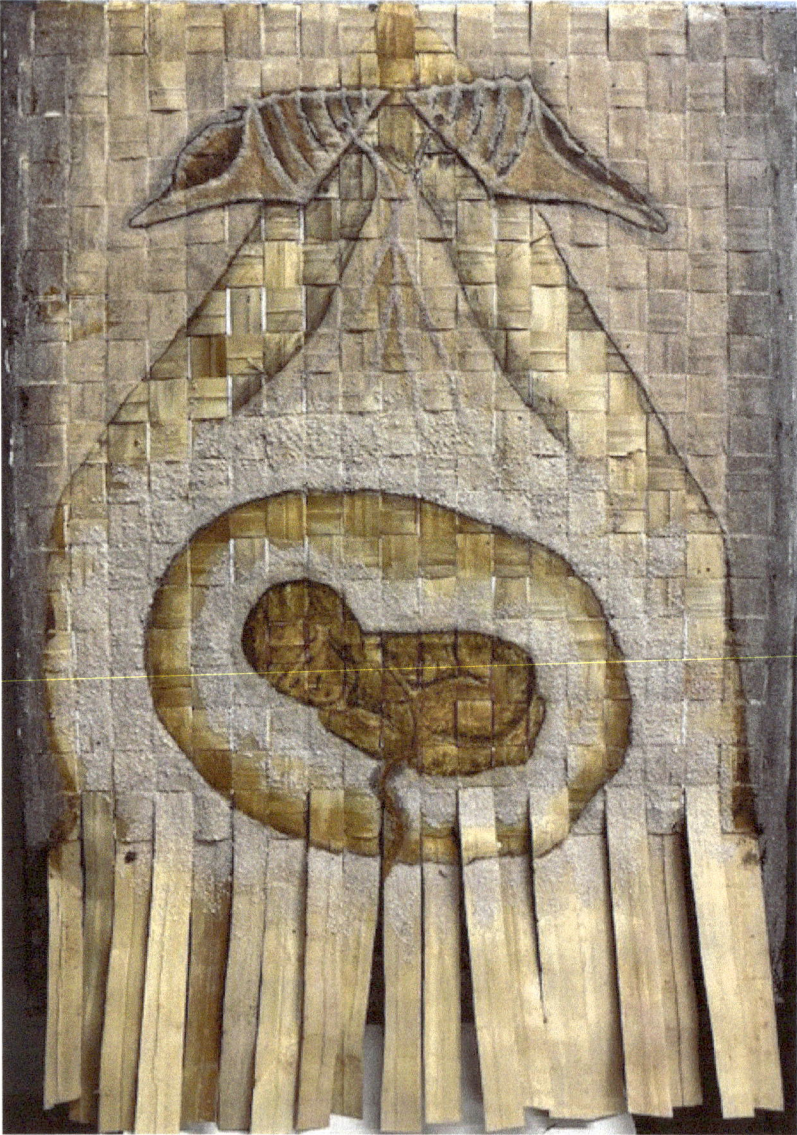

MEANING OF THE FRONT COVER ARTWORK

By McRose Elu

The basket, or woven mat, is what children are born on to and people are placed on to when they pass away. It is used for welcome and farewell. The weaving pattern is an example of the giving and receiving of children, which are interconnected. The umbilical cord from the foetus is buried on the clan land where the child came from. A garden can grow where the cord is buried and acts as a fertiliser for new birth and growth. Traditionally most babies were born in villages in huts made of palm trees and bamboo. The shells at the top of the palm trees have a scared meaning. They are cone shells that talk to the ancestors as well as delivering good news to the community after the baby is born.

FOREWORD

By Alastair Nicholson, former Chief Justice
of the Family Court of Australia

I t is with great pleasure that I write the foreword for this excellent
book written by my friend and colleague, Paul Ban, with whom I
have worked for many years on the Working Party of Torres Strait
Islanders in relation to the obtaining of legal recognition of their
customary child rearing practice.

The practice is discussed in detail in the book, but by way of
introduction it can be said that it involves the giving of children
from one family to another, often as quickly as possible after birth or
at a very young age, but the giving can also occur later. The children
are thereafter treated as members of the receiving family, and they
are not told who their birth parents are until much later or, in a few
cases, not at all.

This practice has in the past been referred to as 'traditional adoption', but that term is avoided in the new legislation, because it causes
confusion with sometimes negative concepts of western adoption.

The practice has been followed by Torres Strait Islanders since time immemorial as a most significant part of their culture. Paul Ban points out that this is part of the notion of extended family integral to Torres Strait Islander culture. It is also worth noting that similar practices are widespread throughout the Pacific, including Papua New Guinea, New Zealand, Hawaii and the Pacific's many other islands. They also occur in parts of the USA and Canada.

It is interesting to note that despite the widespread nature of the practice, it has to date received little legal recognition in the Pacific. Papua New Guinea is the only Pacific country to have legislated to approve the practice, although legislation is being considered elsewhere.

In the Canadian province of Nunavut, a similar practice has been legally recognised for many years and legal recognition can be given by a commissioner and not a court, as it now can in Queensland. In fact, the Canadian precedent was in part adopted in drafting the Queensland legislation.

Similarly, the practice is widespread amongst Indian tribes in British Columbia and have been widely recognised by the courts of that province.

THE TORRES STRAIT ISLANDERS' WORKING PARTY

This Working Party has been the prime mover in gaining support for the legal recognition of the new legislation. It is important to bear in mind this was a truly Torres Strait Islander exercise, led by Islanders. The role of some whites such as Paul and myself has been a lesser and advisory one. We have, however, also been able to help them gain the attention of government to the issue.

The result of the exercise, which has continued for over thirty years, has been the passage by the Queensland Parliament of the *Meriba Omasker Kaziw Kazipa Act* in 2021. Apart from the unique subject matter of the Act, it has the distinction of being the first Act passed by the parliament where the title is in each of the languages of the Torres Strait Island peoples. The language is derived from Eastern and Top Western languages and translates into English as 'For our children's children'.

It is also important to note that this Act has also been, what we believe to be, the first legislation by any Australian Government to formally recognise Indigenous customary law as part of the law of a state or territory.

It has been a long and difficult struggle to achieve this result, as this book makes clear. It pays tribute to the leadership of the late Uncle Steve Mam, who founded the Working Party and worked tirelessly to produce the outcome that has been achieved. He enlisted my support in 1993, when I paid the first of many visits to the islands. He was a fascinating speaker in both his own language and English, and completely dedicated to this cause. It was particularly sad that he died before the result had been achieved, albeit that this outcome was by that time well in sight.

Uncle Steve was succeeded as the chair of the Working Party by Aunty Ivy Trevallion, who was a long-time member of it. She has proved to be a worthy successor, whose advocacy did much to achieve its success with the Queensland Parliamentary Committee that reported favourably to the Queensland Parliament, prior to the passage of the Act.

The Working Party is now an official advisory committee to the Queensland Government but keeps its independence from government. It meets regularly with the newly appointed commissioner and staff together with Queensland Government representatives.

This book is a fitting tribute to the courage and dedication of all involved in achieving what I believe to be an historic result.

Steve Mam

ODE AND DEDICATION TO A LEADER – EZRA STEPHEN LEO MAM (ESLM)

By Bill Lowah

His favourite saying was 'Give me a fowl house and I'll build you a castle' … Herein lies the indomitable character of a human being. ESLM was a man who experienced all the torments, traumas and triumphs that life can conjure. His zest for life was evidenced by his unclouded acceptance, knowing who he is and where he come from. His was the intimate understanding based on cultural integrity, family, and life's journey itself.

It was because of the simple task of responding to a mother's call for help (Aka Rizah) regarding her grandchildren that Steve set about on a lifelong journey to recognise Torres Strait Islander customary law practices of child rearing – giving a child and accepting a child, similar to Western adoption. He wanted to respond as quickly as he could to a grandmother's plea rather than be caught up in governmental processes.

He was the inspiration and author, depicted through the life cycle of a coconut palm tree as 'A Metaphor for Torres Strait Islander Life' – a cultural, spiritual explanation of a Torres Strait Islander person's life from birth to death to life. This has become an intriguing and intellectual interest of his people and many non-Torres Strait Islander commentators and researchers alike.

These pages, from cover to cover, reflect the leadership and determination of Steve to achieve the cry for help from Aka Rizah. His aim was realised when the Meriba Omasker Kaziw Kazipa legislation was proclaimed – after many, many years – in July of 2021 as an Act of parliament in Queensland.

This made Torres Strait Islander cultural child rearing practices legal.

This enduring journey was started by him, and it is his legacy that continues to inspire us all and gives credit to all involved where credit is due. This ode is a commemoration to his commitment, to his family, his loved ones, his friends – and his life's work.

INTRODUCTION

When the Australian federal and state governments talk about engaging with Aboriginal or Torres Strait Islander people regarding issues such as health, housing, child welfare, juvenile justice, adult offending and a range of other social services, the official mantra is that the implementation of service delivery needs to be led by Indigenous people, with government responding. The opposite is usually the case. Governments design programs FOR Indigenous people and try and engage them in a partnership that is government led and managed.

This book is about the remarkable achievement of a group of Torres Strait Islanders, who remained together as a group for over thirty years, lobbying the Queensland Government to achieve legal recognition of their customary child rearing practice. The issue was led by Torres Strait Islanders, with the support of some white professionals, and was neither understood nor considered a government priority for over thirty years. Torres Strait Islanders made submissions to the Queensland Government in the belief that there would be a positive response to an issue that was important to them and led by them.

The child rearing practice has some similarities to the western concept of 'adoption' of children. However, children are not placed with strangers, or non-relatives, after approval by white professionals. They are placed within the wider extended family for a number of reasons by family members themselves. Children are shared within families in the community and create strong bonds between the giving family and the receiving family. The term 'adoption' was coined by anthropologists after they recorded the widespread custom throughout the Pacific and among the Inuit people of Canada. White professionals working for the Queensland Government had great difficulty comprehending a practice that was fundamentally different to the western notion of 'adoption', with which they were familiar.

The reason the achievement is remarkable is because it has been a David and Goliath struggle, with Torres Strait Islanders being Australia's Indigenous minority: 10% of the total Indigenous population, which is only 4% of the Australian population. Due to the remote location of their homelands, between the tip of Cape York and Papua New Guinea, they are out of sight and out of mind of the average Australian.

As this custom is not one easily understood by white government professionals, the request by Torres Strait Islanders for legal recognition has been a long journey of misunderstandings and procrastination by the Queensland Government. In September 2020 the Meriba Omasker Kaziw Kazipa (Torres Strait Islander Child Rearing Practice) Bill was introduced into parliament by the first Torres Strait Islander to become a member of parliament. The Bill was proclaimed as legislation on 1 July 2021, a day Torres Strait Islanders commemorate as 'The Coming of the Light'. This is an auspicious date for Torres Strait Islanders, as on 1 July 1871 the London Missionary Society arrived on Erub (Darnley) Island. Torres Strait Islanders were able to successfully integrate their spiritual beliefs with those of Christianity. Many Torres Strait Islanders believe that the passing of legislation on this date has a spiritual significance.

This book will initially explain the custom from a Torres Strait Islander perspective. Those outside Ailan Kastom, and who are not Torres Strait Islanders, have found it difficult to understand a practice based on collectivist and communal ways of living rather than western individualism. The fact that the Queensland Government was able to finally pass legislation to support an Indigenous custom that they have always had difficulty understanding underlines how the achievement has happened from a seemingly impossible situation and against all odds.

CUSTOMARY ADOPTION – AN ANTHROPOLOGICAL UNDERSTANDING

From Paul Ban, 'Traditional Adoption Practices of the Torres Strait Islanders and Qeensland Adotption Legislation.' Master of Social Work thesis, University of Melbourne, 1989.

Customary adoption is a widespread practice that involves all Torres Strait Islander extended families in some way, either as direct participants or as kin to adopted children. It should not be confused with the Aboriginal Stolen Generations' experience of white authorities taking children from their family networks and placing them in white families (*Bringing Them Home Report*, 1997). Adoptions are arranged between relatives and close friends where bonds of trust and reciprocity have already been established. There is no 'assessment' and 'approval' by an independent and usually white authority.

Some of the reasons for the widespread nature of adoption include:

- Maintaining the family bloodline by adopting (usually) a male child from a relative. This is linked to the inheritance of traditional land in the islands.
- Keeping the family name by adopting a male child from a relative or close friend into the family.
- Giving a family who cannot have a child due to infertility the joy of raising a child. A married couple may give a child to either a single person or another couple. 'Relinquishment' is not restricted to single parents.
- Strengthening alliances and bonds between the two families concerned.
- Distributing boys and girls more evenly between families who may only have children of one sex.
- Replacing a child who has been adopted out to another family. This may occur within extended families.
- Replacing a child into the family once a woman has left home so that the grandparents would still have someone to care for.

The most common way an adoption takes place is for a woman who is pregnant to make a promise to the potential adoptive parents that the child will belong to them from the time of birth. The underlying principle of Torres Strait Islander adoption is that it cannot be assumed that a birth parent will always be the parent who raises the child. The issue of who raises the child is dependent on a number of social factors such as those listed and is a matter of individual consideration by the families involved. Children are not lost to their birth family as they are usually given to relatives or close friends within their kinship and social network.

The main characteristics of Torres Strait Islander customary adoption are:

- It provides a sense of stability to the social order and is seen as having a useful social function.
- It is characterised by the notions of reciprocity and obligation between the families involved.
- It generally occurs within the wider network of the extended family and carries with it the intention of permanency.
- It occurs frequently but can have an element of instability and fragility, sometimes leading to its dissolution following disputes between families over the care of the child.

CUSTOMARY ADOPTION AS EXPLAINED BY TORRES STRAIT ISLANDERS

Quotes and excerpts from *Public Hearing – Inquiry into the Meriba Omasker Kaziw Kazipa (Torres Strait Islander Traditional Child Rearing Practice) Bill 2020*, Transcript of Proceedings. Health, Communities, Disability Services and Domestic and Family Violence Prevention Committee, 7 August 2020.

THE WOVEN MAT

Mayor Phillemon Mosby, Warraber Island:

For Torres Strait Islanders, the mat signifies life's journey from cradle to grave. It is used for housing material, sleeping, conceiving, birthing, initiation, education, marriage, welcoming, meeting, transport, hunting, ceremonies, shelter and to our final journey. The interwoven pattern and the weaving of our mat signifies our strength and our unity in any challenges we face, but most importantly in this context it signifies the interconnection of all Torres Strait Islanders, regardless of which island or community we may originate from. We are all interconnected, and the residents of our community are all interrelated.

Ms Cynthia Lui MP, Yam Island:

When we talk about the interconnectedness of our people with each other, it represents that mat because, unlike the westernised society, we are all connected either through blood or simply because of our very existence in these communities. Each of us are related to each other. That is important for us to understand. That is why we are supporting this, and that is why people could not understand before. We are all cousins, mothers, fathers, grandfathers.

Mr Ezra Anu, from Saibai Island, shared a Western Islander view of Torres Strait child rearing practices:

From a Western Island perspective in regards to island adoption, we hold the family circle as very important. In non-Indigenous family circles there is a mother, a father and two or three children. With our family it extends out to uncles, aunties and grandparents.

For our community, the waku, the mat that we play on and sit on, is regarded as an analogy of family and community. The strands are woven together which holds our family together. Our relationship with each other and other clan groups is very important and vital. This legislation will legitimise that law in regard to our recognition of island adoption. I am a product of that. That means that we adopt inside of our totems.

Aunty Ivy Trevallion explained that in the Western Islands of the Torres Strait it is custom:

... particularly with women, if we marry out, we have to replace ourselves back in the family. So, the eldest child usually is the one that we place with the family. Another one is that if you have a child out of wedlock the family would raise the child for you. Women in particular are not subjected to any sort of domestic violence or jealousy of any sort. The woman can then walk her life knowing that this child is safe with the family group who would look after it.

... The Eastern Islanders practice mainly through the blood lines, so you must be related to that person or family for them to give you a child. With the Western Islands, you can transfer the child.

Uncle Francis Tapim, an Eastern Islander, explained:

In Mer culture it [the giving of a child] is through the blood line. When we say 'blood line', if I am the brother, Mrs A is the sister and Leo is the child and Mrs A as my sibling has no children, we agree – brother and sister agree – to adopt Leo. That is what we mean by through blood line, because we are related through blood.

17

We are siblings. We are first cousins. Cousins are recorded in that with siblings.

The notion of the extended family is integral to Torres Strait Islander culture. A broad view is held about who is included in family and the role played by this extended family, particularly in relation to child rearing 'for transmitting traditional values and skills and other cultural practices, and for ensuring continuity of moral precepts and behaviour'.

Torres Strait Islander traditional custom 'involves the shared responsibility of raising children with family and close friends with whom bonds have already been established'. This shared responsibility includes a 'sacred cultural practice' which:

> ... supports the permanent transfer of parentage for a child from the biological parents to the cultural parents in accordance with Ailan Kastom. It is a consent based verbal agreement that usually occurs within an extended family. Under the practice, the child's biological parents are never lost to a child as the child is usually placed within the family network. The child continues to have a relationship with them and can recognise them as aunt, uncle or another familial relationship.
>
> The practice is an integral part of Torres Strait Islander community and family life, is strongly connected to wider aspects of customary law and is important to the sense of stability and social order of Torres Strait Islander society.

When introducing the Bill, Ms Cynthia Lui, the Member for Cook, described the practice as:

... an ancient, sacred and enduring child-rearing practice, an integral part of Torres Strait Islander cultural fabric since time immemorial. This practice sits on the foundations of Torres Strait Islander culture and cultural decision-making processes in Torres Strait Islander community and family life. It promotes inclusiveness by allowing children the ability to grow into their full potential without doubt or questions about their identity.

The concept of transferring children differs between western and Torres Strait Islander ideology. Aunty Ivy Trevallion explained, 'The western ideology is about ownership, whereas with Indigenous, with us, it's about sharing.'

The term 'Kupai Omasker' has been given to traditional adoption in government and legal circles as it derives from the name of the Working Party established to advocate for legal recognition of the practice. The following describes how the term was developed:

In recognition of the diversity of languages in the Torres Strait and the commonality of the practice across language groups, the working group agreed upon the term Kupai Omasker to describe the Torres Strait Islander traditional adoption project. 'Kupai' is the Torres Strait Western Islands word for 'umbilical cord' and 'Omasker' is the Torres Strait Eastern Islands word for 'children'. The words used together can be interpreted as 'the caring of all our children'. In time it has come to be used as a term for the traditional adoption practice facilitating a common understanding of Torres Strait Islanders and non-Torres Strait Islanders.

Mr Elimo Tapim explained:

> *We say that we are Torres Strait Islanders. We have culture. We are different in culture. We have eastern group culture and also western group culture. They are culturally not different but similar.*

Aunty Edna Mark commented on the commonalities shared by Torres Strait Islanders, whether they live in the Torres Strait or on the mainland of Australia:

> *There are certain cultures for certain groups. There is a difference, but it all points to the same thing – some sort of recognition of cultural adoption. It is a hard road that everybody has travelled.*

The Torres Strait Island Regional Council Mayor Phillemon Mosby stated:

> *This is not about being recognised in our communities, that recognition already existed, this is more so for our children to reaffirm their identity and place in a western society.*
>
> *As Torres Strait Islanders, we are all inter-connected and residents of our communities are all inter-related. Because of our inter-connectedness, adoption for Torres Strait Islanders takes on a different context to that in the western world. So too does extended family and kinship.*

TWO PRESS RELEASES

Cynthia Lui, Torres Strait Islander and Member for Cook (Cape York And The Torres Strait) and The Premier of Queensland, Annastacia Palaszczuk.

Historic day for Torres Strait Islanders and Queensland Parliament
24 July 2020

CYNTHIA LUI MP
MEMBER FOR COOK
MEDIA RELEASE

LEGISLATION introduced into the Parliament last week recognises that Torres Strait Island children and adults who have grown up with traditional adoptive parents will have their legal identity match their cultural identity.

In presenting the historic bill, the Member for Cook, Cynthia Lui, a proud Iamalaig woman from the Kulkalgal Tribe of the Torres Strait, said this was an important and historic event in Queensland's history.

The Meriba Omasker Kaziw Kazipa (Torres Strait Islander

Traditional Child Rearing Practice) Bill, introduced on Thursday, July 16, delivered on Labor's 2017 election commitment.

For generations, Torres Strait Islanders have supported their children and each other in loving, supportive extended families.

'But these family relationships were not fully recognised in Australian law,' Ms Lui said.

'The introduction of this bill puts us one step closer to realising this long-fought recognition.

'This bill provides legal recognition of an ancient, sacred and enduring child-rearing practice, an integral part of Torres Strait Islander cultural fabric since time immemorial.

'This practice sits on the foundations of Torres Strait Islander culture and cultural decision-making processes in Torres Strait Islander community and family life.

'It promotes inclusiveness by allowing children the ability to grow into their full potential without doubt or questions about their identity.'

Ms Lui said many generations of Torres Strait Islander children had been raised under the traditional practice which protected a person's cultural right and identity and their position in the family, kinship and community structure.

'Children who are raised under this practice deserve only love, respect, dignity and acceptance, and the questions about who they are and where they come from are irrelevant,' she said.

'This practice ensures that the child's cultural right is treated with the utmost respect and dignity they deserve.'

'The new law will be based on three guiding principles – consent of biological parents, recognition of the birth parents' assessment of the suitability of the cultural parents, and the rights and best interests of the child throughout their life.

'This bill is about the preservation and survival of *ailan kastom* (island custom) by providing a legal framework to support the recognition of Torres Strait Islander traditional child-rearing practice, which has occurred since time immemorial.

'In accordance with international and Queensland human rights standards, this bill therefore honours *ailan kastom* and promotes Torres Strait Islander cultural rights, including the right to practice their own laws, customs and traditions, and the right to self-determine their own identity.

'Legal recognition of the traditional child-rearing practice will allow Torres Strait Islander people to access fundamental human rights, for example, important identity documents, such as a birth certificate, which allow for easy access to government services such as financial support and school enrolment benefits that most Queenslanders take for granted.

'This sacred cultural practice supports the permanent transfer of parentage for a child from the biological parents to the cultural parents in accordance with ailan kastom.

'It is a consent-based verbal agreement that usually occurs within an extended family.

'Under the practice, the child's biological parents are never lost to a child as the child is usually placed within the family network.

'The child continues to have a relationship with them and can recognise them as aunt, uncle or another familial relationship.

'A cultural recognition order made under this bill will result in a new birth certificate being issued to the person who is the subject of the application.

'Being able to obtain a key identification document like a birth certificate which reflects a person's cultural identity will result in many positive flow-on effects, such as access to government services and school enrolments.

'All decisions under the bill, including deciding to make a cultural recognition order, must be for the wellbeing and best interests of a person who is the subject of an application for a cultural recognition order, either children or adult children applicants.

'The bill sets out a voluntary, opt-in, consent-based process.

'In the case of a child who is the subject of an application, consent for legal recognition must be provided by the biological parents and cultural parents where reasonably and appropriately available.

'In the case of adult applicants who were once children under the practice they, too, must provide consent in the application.

'Suitability of the cultural parents means that the cultural practice has occurred and has been verified by persons with knowledge and understanding of the cultural practice specific to the community.

'The verification process is part of the application, and it allows for those informed persons to verify that the practice has occurred. The commissioner will have discretion to seek criminal history information about the cultural parents if required.

'This is to ensure an appropriate level of safeguards is in place and is consistent with other legislative frameworks which consider the best interests and wellbeing of children.'

The bill will commence on a day to be fixed by proclamation, and implementation is scheduled for operation in the first half of 2021.

What's in a name?

- The short title of the Meriba Omasker Kaziw Kazipa (Torres Strait Islander Traditional Child Rearing Practice) Bill contained Torres Strait Islander languages.

- Derived from Eastern and Top Western languages, Meriba Omasker Kaziw Kazipa translates as 'For our children's children'.
- The phrase pays homage to the legacy of the Kupai Omasker Working Party, formed in 1990 by the late Uncle Steve Mam.
- The Kupai Omasker Working Party advocated for the legal recognition of Torres Strait Islander traditional child-rearing practice for more than 30 years.

Torres Strait Islander families a step closer to legal recognition

Published Thursday, 16 July 2020 at 03:36 PM

PREMIER AND MINISTER FOR TRADE
THE HONOURABLE ANNASTACIA PALASZCZUK

An historic day in State Parliament today (Thursday 16 July), after new legislation was introduced that brings Torres Strait Islander families and communities in Queensland a step closer to legal recognition of the traditional child rearing practices.

Torres Strait Islander and Member for Cook, Cynthia Lui today introduced a Private Member's Bill, Meriba Omasker Kaziw Kazipa (Torres Strait Islander Traditional Child Rearing Practice) Bill 2020.

This Bill was introduced with the full support of the Palaszczuk Government and was adopted by the Government.

The Premier said for generations, Torres Strait Islanders have supported their children and each other in loving supportive extended families, but these family relationships have not been fully recognised in law.

'This legislation means children and adults who have grown up with traditional adoptive parents will finally have their legal identity match their cultural identity, supporting and strengthening their connection to community and culture,' the Premier said.

'I know this is an issue close to the heart of the Member for Cook Cynthia Lui and it would never have happened without her as the first Torres Strait Islander being elected to Queensland Parliament.

'Not only is this nation leading but it's world leading, and this is very important and proud day for the people of the Torres Strait.'

Torres Strait Islander leadership has been advocating to have this cultural practice legally recognised for more than 30 years. It aims to bridge the gap between traditional lore and western law for caregivers and children from extended Torres Strait Islander families.

The Minister for Fire and Emergency Services and Minister for Aboriginal and Torres Strait Islander Partnerships, Craig Crawford today introduced the Bill.

'Queensland is leading the nation with the Meriba Omasker Kaziw Kazipa Bill 2020 on-track to become the first legislation of its kind in Australia,' Mr Crawford said.

'The Queensland Government has partnered with Torres Strait Islander communities to deliver on its election commitment supported by a $1 million investment delivered over three years to support this historic outcome.

'It is important our contemporary legal system evolves to recognise, accommodate and celebrate the diversity of Queensland families.'

Torres Strait Ministerial Champion Shannon Fentiman has met with families across the Torres Strait and heard directly from them about the importance of this legislation to them and their culture.

'This is an historic piece of legislation that will ensure Torres Strait Islander children and adults who have been part of this traditional family structure can have their legal identity match their cultural identity,' Ms Fentiman said.

'This will mean they will be able to do things we take for granted such as having a passport in their own name or being able to obtain a drivers licence.'

Minister for Child Safety, Youth and Women Di Farmer said cultural background and identity were integral to the wellbeing of children.

'The translation of Meriba Omasker Kaziw Kazipa is for our children's children, but today it means so much more as we acknowledge the enduring culture that unites Torres Strait Islander families and communities,' Ms Farmer said.

A panel of Eminent Persons with legal and cultural expertise – Ms Ivy Trevallion; former Chief Justice of the Family Court of Australia the Honourable Alastair Nicholson; and Mr Charles Passi – led extensive community consultation ahead of the Bill's introduction to State Parliament.

The Queensland Government's role is to establish a legislative framework that recognises the cultural practice – not to determine whether the cultural practice should or should not have occurred.

THE TORRES STRAIT AND ITS ISLANDS

The Torres Strait is named after a Spanish navigator and captain, **Luís Vaz de Torres**, who was the first European to sail through Torres Strait in 1606 on his way to Manila in the Philippines, 150 years before Captain Cook. It is the waterway separating far northern Australia (Cape York Peninsula) and New Guinea, between the Arafura Sea in the east and the Coral Sea in the west.

The Torres Strait Islands are a group of over 200 small islands, distributed across an area of around 48,000 square kilometres. At its narrowest point the area extends around 150 kilometres from north to south, and at its widest point around 300 kilometres from east to west.

Not all islands belong to Australia, only those that lie within 60 nautical miles (97 kilometres) north from the coast of Cape York.

In August 1770, Captain Cook took possession of Australia's east coast in the name of King George III on Bedanug, an island he named Possession Island. In 1879 Queensland annexed the islands which put them under the control of the same policies of protection and segregation as the rest of Australia.

Without consultation, former Prime Minister Gough Whitlam in the 1970s proposed to move Australia's northern border with Papua New Guinea south, effectively cutting in half the area of the Torres Strait Islands. But his proposal was unsuccessful, and a new conservative government signed a treaty with Papua New Guinea in December 1978, maintaining the original border.

TORRES STRAIT ISLAND GROUPS

Map showing the five Torres Strait Island groups. Each group has similar geology, ecology and location.

Culturally, the islands are divided into five groups, represented by the five-pointed star on the Torres Strait flag. Each has similar characteristics for geology, formation and location:

- **Northern Islands** (also called Top/North Western [Gudamaluilgal] Islands). Also known as the hunting islands, they are drier, low-lying larger islands with abundant wildlife, formed by deposition of sediments and mud from New Guinean rivers, close to the south-western coastline of New Guinea.

    Includes: Saibai, Boigu (Talbot Island), Dauan (Mt Cornwallis Island), Warul Kawa (Deliverance Island).

- **Western Islands** (also called Near/Lower Western [Malvilgal] Islands). Also known as the rocky islands, they lie south of the Strait's midway point, largely consisting of high granite hills with basaltic outcrops, formed from old peaks of the now submerged land bridge, an extension of the Great Dividing Range.

    Includes: Moa (Banks Island), Badu (Mulgrave Island), Mabuiag (Jervis Island), Pulu Islet, Nagi (Mt Ernest Island).

- **Southern Islands** (also called Inner [Kaiwalagai] Islands). They lie closest to Cape York Peninsula and host most of the population. Some have permanent freshwater springs and have been centres of pearling and fishing industries. Their inhabitants have a strong connection to mainland Aboriginal people.

    Includes: Muralag (Prince of Wales Island), Waiben (Thursday Island), Ngurupai (Horn Island), Kiriri (Hammond Island), Bedanug or Bedhan Lag (Possession Island).

- **Central (Kulkalgal) Islands**. Also known as the fishing islands, they are widely distributed and most consist of many small sandy cays with little fresh water, surrounded by coral reefs. Some have high basaltic outcrops.

  Includes: Aureed (Skull Island), Gerbar (Two Brothers), Iama (Yam Island), Poruma (Coconut Island), Warraber (Sue Island), Masig (Yorke Island).

- **Eastern (Meriam) Islands.** Also known as the gardening islands, they are the peaks of former volcanoes with rich and fertile red volcanic soils and thick vegetation. Many have historic fish traps along their coastline.

  Includes: Mer (Murray Island), Dauar (Cornwallis Island), Waier, Erub (Darnley Island), Ugar (Stephen Island).

Only seventeen of the islands are inhabited, and only twenty islands have sufficient fresh water for permanent human settlement.

POPULATION STATISTICS

Among the Aboriginal and Torres Strait Islander population in 2011, **6%** (38,100) identified as Torres Strait Islanders only, while another 4% (25,600) were of both Aboriginal and Torres Strait Islander origin.

But not all Islanders live on the Torres Strait Islands. **64%** of them (24,386) live in Queensland, both the mainland state and the islands. Of those, **only 28% (6,885) actually live on one of the islands**. The remainder (17,501) live in communities along the coast of Queensland, particularly Townsville and Cairns, but also Bamaga and Seisia. This phenomenon is sometimes referred to as the 'Torres Strait diaspora'.

Most islands have populations of between 100 and 200 people.

Torres Strait Islanders live in all states and territories of Australia, in urban, regional and remote areas, where they might practice their Islander culture. The **majority live in Queensland and New South Wales**, but there are also large communities in Victoria and Tasmania.

According to Australian Bureau of Statistics figures from the 2021 census, there are approximately **69,895** Torres Strait Islander people in Australia. Those identifying as being of Aboriginal and/or Torres Strait Islander origin were **812,728** people, representing **3.2%** of the total population. Of the Aboriginal and Torres Strait Islander people counted, **91.4%** identified as Aboriginal; **34,135**, or **4.2%**, identified as Torres Strait Islander; and **35,760**, or **4.4%**, identified as both Aboriginal and Torres Strait Islander.

According to the 2021 census, there are approximately **5,913** Torres Strait Islanders living in the Torres Straits. A total of **1,684** people identifying as Aboriginal and/or Torres Strait Islander live on Thursday Island.

Torres Strait Islander culture is also known as 'Ailan Kastom'.

ORIGINS

More than 8,000 years ago, sea levels were about 100 metres lower than today and much of the Torres Strait formed a land bridge between Papua New Guinea and Australia. It helped people move from southern New Guinea to Cape York. Some animal and bird species which live in both Papua New Guinea and North Queensland (e.g., the Spotted Cuscus and Southern Cassowary) are evidence of this connection.

Archaeologists found evidence of human settlement dating back **at least 2,500 years**, but this might change if they discover older sites. Archaeologists agree that evidence may be found in the future that dates settlement **up to 4,000 years ago**. Like mainland Aboriginal history, Torres Strait Islander history grows both ways, into the future and into the past. The problem is that older camp sites Islanders made near the shoreline at a time of lower sea levels are now submerged.

The first inhabitants of the Torres Strait are believed to have migrated from the Indonesian archipelago **70,000 years ago**.

LANGUAGES

The two main traditional languages of the Torres Strait Islands are Meriam Mir (spoken in Eastern Islands) and Kala Lagaw Ya (spoken in Near Western Islands).

Meriam Mir is connected to the Papuan languages and has two regional dialects, Mer and Erub. It is the language of the older inhabitants of some of the Eastern Islands, especially Mer. It is spoken by close to 2,000 Islanders.

Examples: Yawo (goodbye), maiem (welcome), baru (yes), nole (no).

Kala Lagaw Ya, still spoken on the main Western Islands, is linguistically connected to the mainland Aboriginal languages and has four regional dialects, Mabuyag, Kalaw Kawaw Ya, Kawrareg and Kulkalgau Ya. It is spoken by around 3,000 Islanders.

Examples: Yawa (goodbye), sew ngapa (welcome), wa (yes), lawnga (no).

Torres Strait Creole (or Kriol), also known as Ailan Tok, Yumplatok or Broken (Brokin), is a mixture of Standard Australian English and traditional languages. It developed from pidgin English while missionaries were on the islands in the 1850s. It has its own distinctive sound system, grammar, vocabulary, usage and meaning.

Most Torres Strait Islanders speak Creole, as it helps speakers of the other languages communicate with each other, and each island has its own flavour. Islanders speak Creole in daily life and on some local and regional radio programs. Creole also spread to the Cape York Peninsula with the Islanders' migration to the mainland.

Government policies prohibited Torres Strait Islanders from using their traditional languages, just like on mainland Australia, and Islanders lost a lot of culture and language.

IDENTITY

Torres Strait Islander people have to **find their ways within two groups**: one people – the Islanders – and their own, local identity which formed from differing ecological, cultural and historical circumstances.

Some Torres Strait Islander people identify strongly with their 'island' roots, including Papua New Guinea, while others identify with the mainland or home country when discussing their identity.

There is **variety in labels** Torres Strait Islanders are comfortable with, similar to the diversity of names for mainland Aboriginal people. Some people prefer to be called 'Torres Strait Islanders' while others prefer just 'Islanders'. Some people prefer local island names and language names to be used in recognising themselves and their identity, for example Badulaig, which refers to the people and not their link to the land.

Like mainland Aboriginal people, Torres Strait Islanders can have **mixed ancestry**. Theirs is likely to also be South Sea Islander, Samoan, Chinese and mainland Aboriginal.

Unique to Torres Strait Islander families, you can **distinguish their houses** from the street by the traditional medicinal and magic plants which surround them (cassava, taro, sweet potato and bananas), and the clam shells placed near the entrance. People leave their shoes outside on the veranda as they would in the Strait and the floors are covered with woven mats. For Torres Strait Islanders, courtesy and kindness are very important. This is known locally as 'Good Pasin', meaning good fashion or behaving with a degree of sophistication and charm.

We are the mariners, the people who can navigate by the stars to small dots of islands beyond the horizon, 'reading' the wind and tides, the reefs and skies. (George Mye – Darnley Island)

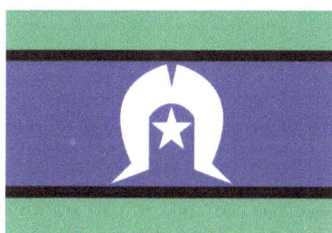

The Torres Strait Islander flag.

The Torres Strait Islander flag was first launched on 29 May 1992. Its colours stand for:

- **Green:** the two mainlands of Australia and Papua New Guinea
- **Blue:** the Torres Strait waters
- **Black lines:** the Torres Strait Islanders
- **Five-pointed star:** the five island groups (Northern, Western, Southern, Eastern and Central Islands)
- **White:** Christianity and peace
- **Dhari head dress:** Islanders and their customs.

KINSHIP

Torres Strait society is organised in **totemic clans**. Totems are the foundation of their culture and can be living creatures, rocks, winds or stars. A clan gives rights and obligations and comes via one's kinship relationships and the connection to land and sea.

HISTORY OF WHITE CONTACT

Due to their relative isolation, following European contact – initially by explorers and later by the London Missionary Society in 1871 – the Queensland Government classified the Strait as a 'reserve' and Torres Strait Islanders were not allowed to leave their homeland and live on the mainland until after World War Two. Consequently, their culture, customs and languages were left reasonably intact and Torres Strait Islander children were not subjected to the forced removal from their families as were Aboriginal Australians throughout the majority of the twentieth century. Although now in the twenty-first century most Torres Strait Islanders live on mainland Australia, they retain a strong connection to their homeland and customs.

Torres Strait Islanders were able to incorporate Christianity into their existing social organisations, with island chiefs becoming church leaders. The hierarchy that controlled social and religious life adapted their pre-contact mode of operating to the new influences brought by European colonisation. The overall effect of these two factors, combined with remaining in their homeland with minimal outside influence, has been that Torres Strait Islanders have not had their culture and customs as negatively impacted as Aboriginal Australians.

Following European contact, the various island communities were identified as a single cultural group by the colonisers. A body of customs, traditions, observances and beliefs, referred to as Ailan

Kastom, has survived European contact and continues through adaptation when under pressure from the imposition of white Australian values and laws. Ailan Kastom forms a strong bond between the different island communities and between Torres Strait Islanders living in the region and on the mainland.

RECENT CONTEXT

During the reign of Premier Joh Bjelke-Peterson and the National Party in Queensland from 1968 to 1987, Torres Strait Islanders were subjected to an assimilationist policy regarding legal recognition of family customary practices. One of the legacies of cultural racism is for governments to pursue policies that advocate everyone should be treated the same by the law, particularly when family cultural practices within communities such as Torres Strait Islanders differ from the white population. This meant that the law that relates to child rearing practices for white Queenslanders is the benchmark for other ethnic and Indigenous groups.

HISTORY OF LEGAL RECOGNITION

Prior to 1985, Torres Strait Islanders were able to have custom adoptions both formalised and legalised by the Queensland Government under adoption legislation used by all Queenslanders. The legalisation took place for administrative simplicity, with there being no attempt by the government to understand and define the practice. Since the early twentieth century the Torres Strait was administered by the Department of Aboriginal and Islanders Advancement, a bureaucracy which managed all the affairs of Aboriginals and Torres Strait Islanders throughout Queensland. It also had the responsibility for making social security payments until the late 1970s and 'rubber stamped' customary adoptions to simplify names for payments.

At regular intervals, the Department of Aboriginal and Islander Affairs simply submitted a list of Torres Strait Islander families to the Department of Children's Services, the department responsible for adoptions, for legal recognition under the relevant adoption legislation at the time. Following the introduction of social workers into the Department of Children's Services in the 1970s, concerns were raised regarding whether 'the best interests' of Torres Strait Islander children were being met by 'rubber stamping' applications with no assessment being undertaken as to the suitability of the future caregivers. In addition, there were concerns about the conditions under which consent was given by birth parents, as they simply had to complete a form and had no counselling.

As there was awareness that customary adoption differed from the definition of 'adoption' in legislation at the time, in the late 1970s the Department of Children's Services intended to commission a study in the Torres Strait of the needs of Torres Strait Islanders regarding legal recognition of customary adoption. It decided not to approve any further customary adoptions until it understood the difference between the two forms of practice. However, the study did not take place, and the Department of Aboriginal and Islander Affairs took the responsibility of 'rubber stamping' customary adoptions from the Department of Children's Services from 1981 to 1985 by stating it was politically embarrassing for the Queensland Government to upset island leaders by delaying their applications.

A political decision was made in 1985 to phase out the Department of Aboriginal and Islander Affairs and for it to give the responsibility of administering Indigenous Queenslanders to the various government departments with individual expertise, such as health, education and welfare. The Department of Children's Services assumed full responsibility for family and child welfare matters, including the legal recognition of customary adoptions. A decision was made to treat customary adoption applications in the same manner as applications by all other Queenslanders who wanted an adoption order. It was decided that no further study would be carried out in the Torres Strait of the difference between customary adoption and 'adoption' as defined in legislation and that Torres Strait Islanders should be discouraged from applying for legal adoption. The policy position was that customary adoption fell outside the parameters of adoption legislation and should not be considered as 'adoption'.

The Kupai Omasker Working Party was formed in the late 1980s and its members have been involved in seeking the legal recognition of customary adoption since 1990. The Queensland Government withdrew the legal recognition it had always given, as far back as records were kept in the Torres Strait, in 1985. Since that decision, Torres Strait Islander children who had been adopted under Island custom did not have a legal relationship with the adults who raised them and who they considered were their parents.

Their practice has different origins and intentions to western adoption and is not a custom practiced by Aboriginal Australians. There are no known records of Torres Strait Islander children being forcibly removed from their families, as with 'half caste' Aboriginal children, and adopted by European/Australian families.

A Master of Social Work thesis was completed by Paul Ban in 1989 on the problems for Torres Strait Islanders due to the Queensland Government's change in policy. There was a change in government in 1989 after twenty-one years of National Party rule. The new Labor Government appeared to be receptive to consultation with Torres Strait Islanders over their desire to have their customary adoption practice legally recognised. Meetings with government along with Torres Strait Islander conferences were held in the early 1990s, where the topic was on the agenda together with land rights and autonomy/self-government in the Torres Strait.

CONSULTATIONS REGARDING THE VIEWS OF TORRES STRAIT ISLANDERS – 1993

A consultancy was commissioned by the Queensland Government in 1993 and funding provided to IINA Torres Strait Islander Corporation, based in Brisbane and led by Steve Mam. IINA contracted Paul Ban to undertake the consultancy because of his thesis on this area. Torres Strait Islanders were interviewed individually as well as together when they attended community meetings. The meetings took place at major towns on the coast of Queensland and six islands in the Torres Strait. A consistent theme throughout the consultation was that, due to the lack of legal recognition of customary adoption, children were being raised in adoptive families and finding out inadvertently that their adoptive name was not the name on their birth certificate.

This caused stress to the children and to the adoptive parents, as under custom children are not told about their adoption until they are considered old enough to understand. Another theme was disputes over estates where the deceased did not leave a will (common among Torres Strait Islanders), as those who were adopted through custom stated they had no legal right to challenge those who were biological offspring. The third major theme was that custom adoption was not legally recognised by the court when disputes arose over the future care of a child who was the subject of an adoption.

The consultancy report contained recommendations regarding options for the Queensland Government to consider and was handed to Minister Anne Warner in 1994 at a Torres Strait Islander ceremonial gathering. Between 1994 and 1999 the Queensland Government relied on advice from the Department of Aboriginal and Torres Strait Islander Policy Development – DATSIPD – regarding how to proceed with the matter. During that time, Rolf Nilsson worked for the policy section of the Department of Children's Services and had made inter-departmental connections with McRose Elu from DATSIPD.

In 1997 a national conference on the legal recognition of customary adoption was funded by the Queensland Government and held in Townsville. Elected Torres Strait Islander representatives confirmed the issues outlined in the 1994 report and confirmed the authority of the Torres Strait Islander Working Party, which was established in 1990, to continue negotiations with the government.

An outcome of that conference was another consultation by the Working Party in 1998 with Torres Strait Islanders in Queensland. Following a national conference and further consultation, various project officers worked on the government's response leading to a discussion paper by the newly named Department of Aboriginal and Torres Strait Islander Policy Development in October 1999.

The discussion paper recommended that a further 'full and proper' consultation take place with the Torres Strait Islander community over proposed ways in which customary adoption could be incorporated legally into existing adoption legislation. Draft legislation was prepared by Michael Limerick, a lawyer working for DATSIPD. However, the Queensland Cabinet received advice from the Member for Cook (Cape York and Torres Strait Region), who was not an Aboriginal or Torres Strait Islander, regarding concerns about aspects of the custom based on representations he stated were made to him by Torres Strait Islanders. Despite the concerns being anecdotal and unverified, the Queensland Government decided not to continue with further consultations regarding draft legislation.

They stated in 1999 that they would refer the matter to the Queensland Law Reform Commission so that customary adoption could be considered together with the legal recognition of other Indigenous customary practices. After repeated inquiries by the Working Party regarding the progress of the matter with the Queensland Law Reform Commission, in 2003 the Queensland Government admitted the matter had not been referred to the commission due to funding disputes between the various government departments involved.

The Queensland Government was reluctant to re-engage with Torres Strait Islanders on the issue any further and did not give any reasons other than it was a low priority.

SURROGACY INQUIRY – 2008

In July 2008 the Working Party were invited by the research director of the Queensland Investigation into Altruistic Surrogacy Committee to make a submission regarding the relevance of their customary adoption practice to the purpose of the inquiry. This had been the only opportunity for dialogue between Torres Strait Islanders and the Queensland Government since 1999. Although the terms of reference stated the inquiry was investigating the decriminalising of altruistic surrogacy and seeking advice as to the role the Queensland Government should play (legally) in regulating such arrangements, among other things, the committee were open to understanding surrogacy from a cross-cultural perspective.

While the other submissions and presentations were from Anglo-European Australians, the Torres Strait Islander presentation highlighted some of the similarities between customary adoption, where a child is often promised to an extended family member during pregnancy, and surrogacy, where two parties make a private and non-commercial arrangement for one party to bear the pregnancy and give birth to a child of part or all biological origin from the other party. The Torres Strait Islander presentation was reported in the Melbourne *Age* (1 July 2008) which stated, 'Committee head Linda Lavarch (former Queensland Attorney-General) said clinics, church groups, the Kupai Omasker Torres Strait Islander Working Group, former Chief Justice of the Family Court Alastair Nicholson, and infertile couples would speak at the hearing.'

Despite the committee showing interest in the Torres Strait Islander practice, in their final report (October 2008) they stated in Recommendation 6 that their custom was outside their terms of reference as it was distinct from altruistic surrogacy and therefore it was not appropriate to consider it in the context of the government's response to the committee's report. A member of the committee, the Member for Barron River in North Queensland, stated in parliament (Hansard, 27 November 2008) following the release of the report, 'the committee would like to see the consideration of the legal status of Torres Strait Islander adoptions squarely placed on the policy agenda. The practice is seen as important in strengthening extended family and continues despite prohibition under surrogacy or adoption law. The committee noted that the Torres Strait Islander traditional practice does not neatly fit with Western notions of adoption and surrogacy.'

ADOPTION LEGISLATION REFORM – 2009

In 2009 the Queensland Government passed an Adoption Bill, after reviewing their 1965 legislation, which stated in Section 7(1) (a) 'because adoption (as provided for in this Act) is not part of Aboriginal tradition or Island custom, adoption of an Aboriginal or Torres Strait Islander child should be considered as a way of meeting the child's need for long term stable care only if there is no better available option.' It noted that 'Island custom includes customary child rearing practice that is similar to adoption in so far as parental responsibility for a child is permanently transferred to someone other than the child's parents. This practice is sometimes referred to as either "customary adoption" or "traditional adoption".'

Consequently, although the Bill acknowledged that Torres Strait Islanders have their own customary adoption practice, for the purposes of the new legislation it fell outside the definition of adoption as outlined in the Bill.

RECOGNITION OF TORRES STRAIT ISLANDER CUSTOMARY ADOPTION IN QUEENSLAND LEGISLATION APART FROM SURROGACY AND ADOPTION

The following Acts all recognise traditional child rearing practices as a result of defining a parent of a Torres Strait Islander child as including a person who **under Island custom** is regarded as parent of the child:

- *Succession Act 1981*, Part 5A
- *Child Protection Act 1999*, Section 11(4)
- *Education (General Provisions) Act 2006*, Section 10(4)
- *Disability Services Act 2005*, Section 78(7)
- *Child Care Act 2002*, Schedule 2

- *Police Powers and Responsibilities Act 2000* (forensic procedures), Schedule 6
- *Freedom of Information Act 1992*, Section 51(4)
- *Public Health Act 2005*, Section 159
- *Health Services Act 1991*, Section 61(4).

None of these statutes sets out a process for determining that Torres Strait Islander customary adoption has taken place but simply recognises its existence.

The *Legislative Standards Act 1992*, Section 4, provides that it is a 'fundamental legislative principle' that 'legislation has sufficient regard to … the rights and liberties of individuals' which depends on, amongst other things, whether legislation 'has sufficient regard to Aboriginal tradition and Island custom'.

SECOND CONSULTATION REGARDING THE VIEWS OF TORRES STRAIT ISLANDERS – 2011/2012

The Working Party made repeated requests to the Queensland Government throughout the majority of the first decade of the twenty-first century to re-open the issue of legal recognition of Torres Strait Islander customary adoption. They approved Alastair Nicholson and Paul Ban to have a face-to-face meeting with the relevant minister, Desley Boyle. As a result, she approved a second extensive consultation in the Torres Strait and on the mainland of Queensland in 2010.

Concerns had been expressed by politicians and public servants throughout that decade that the issues raised in the 1993 consultation might be 'out of date' and that the customary practice might have been modified to such an extent that a different response was needed. The second consultation was undertaken by Queensland

Government employees with expertise in the relevant areas and included the former Chief Justice of the Family Court of Australia, the Honourable Alastair Nicholson. It occurred in the Torres Strait mid-2011 and on the mainland mid- to late-2012.

The Working Party was informed of the outcome of that consultation in October 2013, where the draft report was made available to members of the group and comments sought. There was a remarkable similarity in the outcomes of the two consultancies conducted twenty years apart regarding issues concerning the lack of legal recognition of customary adoption practice. It was noted that although Torres Strait Islanders have been influenced by western concepts of child rearing through television and interaction with the mainland, the practice was integral to Torres Strait Islander cultural identity and would continue despite lack of legal recognition. However, participants still wanted legal recognition, particularly in the form of a new birth certificate that reflected the permanently changed status of the child from being part of the birth, or giving, family, to being part of the receiving, or customary adoptive, family.

The Working Party endorsed this finding and endorsed the community members' comments that the practice was in the best interests of the child. In particular, the Working Party acknowledged the concerns of those interviewed that there was an implication by those outside the cultural practice that the giving of children to extended family, according to custom, might not be in their best interests and should be safeguarded by those who do not understand the practice.

Working Party members with tertiary qualifications in anthropology and linguistics emphasised the difficulty for Torres Strait Islanders in translating English words such as 'giving a child', 'receiving a child', 'relinquishment', 'best interests of a child', 'informed consent' and 'suitability of the receiving parent'. While these terms are widely understood by professionals in the field of adoption and child welfare, Torres Strait Islanders have language terms that reflect principles of reciprocity and obligation between parties and a notion that children's best interests are imbedded within the interests of the society as a whole. Consequently, it is difficult to consider what is in an individual child's best interests without understanding the context of the arrangement.

A particular area of misunderstanding is the notion of confidentiality of the custom, which has led to English interpretations with words such as 'secrecy' and 'taboo', which have negative connotations and misrepresent the intention of the practice. The Working Party has always supported the use of the word 'love' when talking about why the practice takes place and how it operates. They were particularly concerned about the social and emotional harm that had occurred to Torres Strait Islander children since 1985, when the Queensland Government stopped legal recognition of customary adoption in the mistaken belief that there might be something about the custom that they did not understand and that was not in the best interest of children.

An important finding from the second extensive consultation was that there was no mention of young Torres Strait Islander women being pressured to 'relinquish' their babies to 'middle class' Torres Strait Islander families. This 'concern' was raised by the Member for Cook under the previous Labor Government in 1999 and was not found to be the case. It is erroneous to apply the framework of western adoption to a customary practice that is based on strengthening community ties through distributing the responsibility of raising children.

The Working Party believed the Queensland Government had a

responsibility to look after everyone in the state and further believed that there should be a proper legal relationship acknowledged between Torres Strait Islander children currently adopted under custom and the people they consider to be their parents.

WORKING PARTY

interviewed by Paul Ban

TORRES STRAIT ISLANDERS

McROSE ELU

It's been a long, emotional journey. When you first knocked on the door at Queensland University it was a conversation between strangers. You had worked in the Torres Strait and had been living in Cairns.

I come from a big clan of fourteen brothers and sisters and customary adoption was a part of us. I just accepted it and gained loving people. It was a taboo subject, so we didn't talk about it – it just happened. My mother never talked about those things. My father was chieftain in our clan. There were twenty aunties. If you marry into another clan, you put a child back to cover the one that went.

When birth certificates came about, they had the names of the biological parents on them. So, there was a system of telling children about their adoption when they are ready. My story was that I was given as a child, so my aunty said to her daughter one day, 'You give up your picaninny to Rose.'

You were sent to us and went right into our culture. It was relaxing for me personally and gave me a feeling of comfort to be able to talk about things. I felt I could talk to you. You're not a false person and wanted to get really involved and wanted to know more. If I didn't get the right vibes and you weren't for real, I would have closed off. All was revealed from our first meeting. I had mixed emotions talking about it. Our laws were never written and were practiced from time immemorial. But people didn't talk about it. It's about the full cycle of love from family to family.

I had good vibes from our first meeting when I was sussing you out. My father taught me, 'Before you answer, let the person talk and the last sentence of what they said will give you the response to the question.' I didn't see you as a white man. I am trained in anthropology and saw you as a person from another culture. After we talked, I thought, 'What a difference it could make if we could have a new birth certificate but not have the flavour of the culture taken away.' We would still keep practicing our culture.

I felt energised by Steve Mam's strength when he talked about an aunty who lost her adopted children because she was not legally recognised as their mother. Firstly, it was just Steve, you and me – then others came along. We talked about how we were going to tackle the government of the day.

At that time my father was still alive. My mother died in 1977, so he was a father and mother to me. I found strength to talk to him about this topic because he trusted Steve. He said it was a positive subject and said I was old enough to know. He said that there is a white man's law and white men write things down – you have to prove things. He said that things are changing for us – our systems and our lifestyle. He gave his blessing and said, 'You know the good road and the bad road, you can explore this because you come from a big family.' I promised him on his death bed that I would.

Uncle Dana is Dad's cousin and I call him 'Bab', which means 'uncle'. I had already turned you into my brother and felt that God had given me a brother after my late brother passed away. We had a beautiful friendship and relationship. Dad gave him to a cousin as a deacon in the clan group.

He knew the history of our family and would say that there is always light beyond the tunnel. It has been a long tunnel and we did it for thirty years. The scrub was so thick we didn't have enough knives to cut through these branches – but we didn't give up. At one stage the department told us to put it on the shelf.

The other white resource people came to us with their knowledge and spoke their language. God has given us strength to do this, and it has been inspirational that all the strings came together. When we were given bad news from the government in 1999 at the conference on Thursday Island, we weren't going to give up.

We Torres Strait Islanders realised that after we tried to explain our custom, white people found it difficult to understand. They were always looking at it from their own views and used to say, 'How can you give your children away?'

When I spoke to my people, you white resource people were all my references. I could prove you were there for real – I can talk to my people about anything. We built up a friendship and I told my people, 'These white people really want to help us.' I also talked about what was happening between us to lots of groups when I was overseas.

When you tried to understand something, you chose your words carefully so we could feel comfortable. The white resource people showed enthusiasm, wisdom, strength and understanding. You were on the same level as us about how Torres Strait Islanders think.

The people gave us the mandate and the lead to do something and tell the government. The lead was taken by Torres Strait Islanders. We all led the process, and we still work as a team. Ivy is very determined as a leader to make sure the government doesn't separate Torres Strait Islanders from the white resource people. Steve wouldn't have let that happen either. We didn't see you as being different from us and became a team. Some Torres Strait Islanders and some white people have said to get rid of the white resource people. The trust between us and the white resource people was obvious and clear. It helped us build up our energy to see it through. When Steve died, his words were, 'Don't give up, keep going.'

The role of Steve as a leader, and that of Ivy after Steve died, was to provide passion, strength, wisdom and a belief that it can happen. After Steve visited you in Melbourne when you had been sick with cancer, he said to me, 'Bala's going to be alright, he has a strong will to live and see it through.' He told me that you had a fine spirit in you and that you were going to live. We weren't thinking anything bad for you – you were part of this team, and we were going to see it through.

Steve had full trust in Ivy to take over leadership when he couldn't go on. He gave her the opportunity and trusted all of us – Ivy wasn't even hesitant – we are a team forever and ever. He gave us guidance from his hospital bed.

Francis was the floating log and we embraced him back. He missed out on being with us all the way through, but he's back on board now.

This is now the beginning of another journey since the legislation has been passed. It's overwhelming and another step on the road. We are the reference group for the new commissioner. It's now a new birth and a new baby. We are nurturing it and know how to take the first steps – we will overcome obstacles.

IVY TREVALLION

When I was twenty-one and enrolled as a social work student in Brisbane, I was asked to be on the board at IINA Torres Strait Islander Corporation. You came and wanted to talk about Torres Strait Islander adoption, but Bill threw you out. Others said, 'Let's hear him out.' You took a courageous position – it was like throwing a ball into a crocodile pit. It was a topic you normally don't talk about.

Our late leader was a very good community strategist and used community networks and protocols to introduce the subject. He held a number of meetings in Brisbane and some of our community asked why we were talking about this topic. It was an education for our people in the community. We had protests and sit-ins to get the money from the government to hold workshops.

Our late leader took people gently through the process to hold a national Torres Strait Islander workshop in Brisbane in 1991. He was a very good community worker and political strategist and picked a group of the best people to work with him. During the period he was educating the community about the need to legally recognise our custom, he carried the burden on his shoulders of the story of an aunt whose adoption of children broke down.

We came together as a group at an international adoption conference in Melbourne at the end of 1988. A delegation of Torres Strait Islanders went to an adoption and surrogacy conference in New Zealand in 1990 and another delegation went to a Family Court conference in Sydney in 1992. We spoke as a group to the Family Court judges and developed a metaphor for our practice – the Tree of Life. The delegations became the origins of the Working Party, which has stayed together for thirty years.

I have always been interested in customary adoption, as it occurred with my father and lots of my brothers and sisters were adopted. I was given to an uncle and have had other experiences I would like to keep private.

When I did social work and worked as a social worker in child welfare, I realised we would have difficulty practicing our custom and having it legally recognised. Child welfare workers were more interested in hearing about the difficulties children who were adopted under custom were having than talking to me to understand more about the custom.

I thought it was strange when you first wanted to talk about customary adoption. However, when I began hearing about the legal problems, I became interested. The topic is confidential in our custom and I wouldn't have known about the problems if it wasn't for your thesis.

Throughout the thirty years it took to obtain legal recognition, we lobbied whoever we could and spoke at many conferences and meetings. We spoke at the inquiry into surrogacy because the Working Party was already a group, and we were opportunistic in trying to get government to listen to us. We were pushed aside by many politicians. One of the ministers in the 1990s put the issue in the too-hard basket and a Member for Cook told me, 'Ivy, if we do it for you, we have to do it for all the other Australians.' Politicians kept being condescending towards us and after we were told the Queensland Law Reform Commission were looking at it, we later found out they put it on the shelf and didn't do anything. They lied to us.

In the end, we had politicians and public servants who knew exactly what we were talking about. I cried at a meeting with women about the lack of action from government. We Torres Strait Islanders will continue to practice our culture with or without government help. The minister who was the Champion for the Torres Strait knew exactly what had to happen without getting into the details of the cultural practice. She was different from other politicians who tried to muck around with a living culture. Most of the politicians and public servants got nervous and had breakdowns.

You have to take the practice as a whole because of the spiritual aspect of giving and receiving children. When I worked in the child welfare department, I became aware of all the questions that were being asked by the white legal system. In the meantime, my brothers and sisters were having complications after receiving children. The children were coming from family members to family members and arrangements were breaking down and children were being taken back.

Things looked very promising at a Torres Strait Islander national conference on Thursday Island in 1999. The Working Party were endorsed at the conference yet again to represent the wishes of the Torres Strait Islander people when dealing with the government. Draft legislation had been made and Cabinet were considering whether to endorse it while the conference was taking place. However, we were disappointed when the Cabinet said they needed further information and were worried about a backlash.

In order for the white resource people to be able to work closely with us, they had to be adopted into the Torres Strait Islander family as a brother or uncle. We had to understand the white ways in your world so that we could make sense of it in our world – we were teaching each other. We have to make sure and trust that white resource people are not going to use our knowledge to feather their own nest.

Our late chair was angry with the government because they didn't respect that we had a job to do. He recruited all of us and in the end the Working Group was beneficial for the whole Torres Strait Islander community. We had to get community agreement to accept that white resource people were also members of the Working Party. If we didn't understand the law, we would ask you. We would take you with us to government services.

Some public servants and politicians couldn't comprehend what we were talking about. They had their own values and beliefs that influenced their ability to try and understand a practice so foreign to them. The white resource people are a link in the chain to explain things in the world view of white people.

The minister who was the Champion for the Torres Strait, Shannon Fentiman, knew exactly what we wanted, which was a process to adopt a child in their cultural name. People are still shocked because the legislation came about because of the work of people in the community and not the work of the government. We had to educate and teach white people our customs and proto-cols – you have a long way to learn.

We in the Working Party needed to learn from each other. We didn't have any money as a group and had to be opportunistic, making our own arrangements to meet even though we were spread across the country. We didn't have funding or a grant, which helped us keep our independence. There were other special white resource people who came into our lives to help us. When we spoke at confer-ences, we spoke from a Torres Strait Islander perspective by Torres Strait Islanders and from a white perspective by the white resource people.

The thirty-year journey has always been owned by the Torres Strait Islander community. However, you white resource people came in and we worked out how we would work together. You would ask the chair what was acceptable, and we would have a discussion and agreement from the chair first before you spoke to politicians.

The issue of leadership throughout the thirty years is very important to the people. We are in a boat on a dark night among the coral following the stars and constellations to see us through. I have a different style of leadership to the late chair. The period of inspiration he provided has changed and I now just have to guide the boat through the coral reef. My role is to make sure everyone has the opportunity to talk in meetings.

An important breakthrough between us and the government was when the minister who was the Champion for the Torres Strait came to my house on Thursday Island, sat at my table and had a cup of tea. It was very personal, and we discussed a family loss. There is now a link between Aunty Rose, the minister and me as women. Aunty Rose adopted the minister as her daughter. After that connection it was easier for us to talk to her, and it led to the premier coming to Thursday Island to talk to the women. The premier made an election promise to legally recognise our adoption practice – we heard it straight from the horse's mouth.

Everyone at the meeting didn't think it was going to happen, but we knew because we sat in on the original meeting where it was discussed.

Since the legislation has been passed there are queries coming to me from all over the country. Everyone is waiting now to see what happens. During the future meetings between the Working Party and government to help guide the role of the commissioner, we have to decide are we sitting on the doorstep and knocking on the door or are we going to push issues we think are important. Now that the system has stepped in, we have to work out our roles. We in the

Working Party have to be on the same page. We have to be careful that there are no hidden agendas from government.

Native Title Law was written by people who had money. We don't have any money. If we keep asking for money our boat will get stuck on the reef. We want to do things our way and not be imposed on by government people.

Now that we have put the ball down over the try line to score, we need to organise ourselves in the Working Party as a team to make sure we are on the same page and know what the other team could do, such as steal the football. We have had white resource people who seemed like they would be good supporters in the past. However, their boats have become stuck on the reef, and they have not gone with us when needed.

We need to talk about what we have achieved in Queensland, Australia, to other countries like PNG, Canada, Hawaii and New Zealand. All of them have similar issues to us with First Nations people and customary child rearing practices. We need to speak at international conferences and tell the story in a book so that other people can't steal it.

BELZA (Bill) LOWAH

I knew you by name at the start and was wary of 'not another social worker' wanting to 'help' us. Westerners are not the only people in the world and they need to be sussed out. I'm suspicious of white researchers in the medical field and with our art forms. In the past they took our information and used it. If they could do a big PhD, they became bankable. So, you were on trial in the beginning, and rightly so. You were being watched about how you take things in.

The community is my family and my family is the community. We never told each other we were adopted; we just knew who's who in the zoo. We knew who we are and where we fit in. We heard the old people say things, reminding us of our responsibilities to who we are. They told us where the crevices were and what road not to go down. They said it was important for us to maintain our status quo.

We have a village life and it takes a village to raise a child. We have our own projects to maintain our own status quo. White people in the Torres Strait saw it as a passage and weren't concerned about the people. We existed before time, before white arrival. Torres Strait Islanders are funny, they take people for what they do and not what they look like. We look at people's behaviour and not what they own.

For Aboriginal and Torres Strait Islander people to be able to maintain their cultural integrity, the suspicion about whites doesn't have to be said. You're being watched all the time because you haven't been experiencing what we've been experiencing. A saving grace for Torres Strait Islanders is our traditional child rearing practices. The practices are universal and are the cornerstones of our culture. It is like a peg in the ground with a string and plumb attached. The string stops on the circle so we can maintain our bloodline, closeness and harmony.

The child is the lynchpin in disputes between a good and wise decision. These are big issues and are the cornerstone of a leader, hunter/warrior or favourite grandmother. Since 1606 we've seen how different people behave. The English sailors were dirty and stinking when they found good clean water and jumped into it. The water was our drinking water, so it's lucky they weren't crucified. Water is a precious element.

Your learning curve was for us to make sure you didn't jump into the water. I was watching you; we don't put on airs and graces. The judge has had training as well. For Torres Strait Islanders, all the training comes from who we grew up with. They knew who's who and who's connected – we were born with that schooling.

White people don't know who they are. They have been drawn into the web of the Torres Strait Islander community. All of you have a common denominator – you are inquisitive animals born with questions. My peers when I was growing up in white middle-class society didn't worry about who or what they were, but rather what they could get out of a situation.

I was a good athlete at school and when I was in races, I shook every competitor's hand – I was teaching them something. Our education was already there. I was about maintaining cultural integrity for the rest of life's journey.

It was important to see the project through over the thirty-year period. From the date of confinement, the DNA is already written into our future generations. They know who they can go to, run with and talk to – they know they are being watched. Through other people's influences, those things have been damaged. These thirty years provide cultural preservation and hope for time to come.

Steve and I had an unwritten sibling code to look out for each other. When speaking to white people, Steve would hold an audience while I put a bomb under them to see how they behaved. We know why we needed white people. Our 36,000 people will never be able to turn the political screws in our favour. Without you realising it, we exploit you. Your interest is to research and understand. But you have the resources, so we exploit you.

Our marches, sit-ins and demonstrations in the '60s and '70s were very real, with the lynchpin being the land rights issue. Torres Strait Islanders supported our Aboriginal loved ones. When we support them, we support ourselves. We don't have the numbers. Politics is based on numbers, bums on seats. Torres Strait Islanders are 10% of the Indigenous population and now we have legislation that respects our cultural practice.

Māoris only have one language, and even white people can speak it. Torres Strait Islanders have two languages and Creole. Aboriginal people have hundreds of languages, kinship systems, family groups, stories and song-lines. The language that is carried can be dissected and the dialect can change over time to change its meaning in the regions. In the Torres Strait, those from the Eastern Islands and Western Islands can speak each other's languages, as well as Creole.

The leadership of the Working Party was clearly led by Steve, whose control and immense humility is uncanny. Steve and I would prepare you white resource people when we realised we had something you needed to understand. We are walking encyclopaedias on what happens between people. We know what information we have and we feed it to you little by little to make you feel you have more to learn. It's what we teach you.

You fellas have to write these things down. We don't have to write things down; it's within us. You have to write things down for posterity, but we don't have to prove who we are. We need to maintain our cultural integrity, not improve it. Cultural attachments linger longer through our speech. Our metaphors are part of our DNA.

Steve would always phone you for a reason. He had things stewing in his mind and knew what had to be taken into account. He knew his agenda and knew when you needed to contact other white people.

Now that the legislation is passed and a commissioner has been appointed, we in the Working Party don't wipe our hands from this project. We can't stop because we have an integral functional role for the next three years to ensure the integrity, cultural, social and historical aspects are maintained. While politicians are worried about their jobs, our job is to be a safety net for the commissioner and the commissioner's office. Politicians and public servants can't do it.

The Working Party is loose enough to go beyond the call of duty to maintain the balance between community and government. We need to maintain attachments as the inner circle. We have to be loose, but we can tighten up in our own ranks. The key qualities are looseness, flexibility, and independence, being mainly accountable to the community. In the past the identity of the Working Party has been questioned, but now it has an official role.

The logic of government in the past was 'if we do it for you, we have to do it for everyone else.' However, our people have gone before us to maintain family integrity. The minister who was Champion for the Torres Strait was effective whereas other politicians said the right thing but did nothing. She is a learned white woman who knows she has to listen intently so she and others like her don't look foolish. They have to look like they know something others don't know.

Just as each player on a football field knows their role, the minister and other women who are politicians of a same age with similar political, social and educational background, have an under-standing and don't have to say words. We went through so many ministers who said they didn't want to give Torres Strait Islanders special privileges. It has been a long road and we have to remember how we got to where we are today.

FRANCIS TAPIM

Customary adoption was in my family. When I came to Townsville from Murray Island I worked as a social worker with ACCA (the Aboriginal Child Care Agency). There were problems with birth certificates and they still had the biological parents' names on them. This was in the 1970s and early 1980s. The children needed birth certificates for sports and passports to verify who they were. When they saw the birth certificate, they started asking questions of their adoptive parents.

I was the chairman of the National Secretariat of Torres Strait Islanders and customary adoption was always on the agenda. People could make comments about it. It was very common in my family, and it is fair to say that every Torres Strait Islander family has been affected by customary adoption.

I was on the Working Party at the beginning, with Uncle Steve Mam, Uncle Belza, Aunty McRose and Uncle Dana – Ivy came later. There were meetings in Brisbane organised by Steve and public servants. My role was to represent the Eastern Torres Strait Islands as well as the Chairman of the National Secretariat. The topic was on the agenda every year at Torres Strait Islander conferences. Uncle Steve was nominated as a spokesperson, along with Uncle Belza (Bill) and Aunty McRose.

There was a Torres Strait Islander conference in Townsville in the 1990s on the need to legally recognise customary adoption. The Working Party was endorsed again at that conference.

I came back to join the Working Party because I found the motivation and energy to stay with the topic. It is important to make sure customary adoption is recognised. My family is involved and there was a thing inside my head that I needed to fix up. My father was adopted and when an issue came up with his adopted grandmother, she told him to go back and see his biological family. His father had to bring all his brothers together and he changed his name from Marou to Tapim.

The thing that kept me going was that customary adoption was not legally recognised, it was just Ailan Kastom. Uncle Eddie Mabo's adoption on Murray Island was not recognised by the court as an adoption to the Mabo family. It wasn't recorded and only acknowledged by the families who were there to see the adoption take place.

We had no knowledge of what the white man was going to think about our adoption practice. We talk in a different language to the white man's English and it is difficult to put our language into white man's language. We respected the white resource people who helped us gain insight into the legal structure. You were seen as professionals who could offer assistance and you were invited to help us.

Uncle Steve was the leader and chair of the Working Party. He was able to steer us and to take professional advice. When we started working with white people we had to see if we could work together. We Torres Strait Islanders go on trust and rely on our hearts to decide if someone in genuine.

I have seen changes to laws for gay people to be able to adopt and to marry and for white people to practice surrogacy. However, Torres Strait Islander adoption is a separate issue, and the government didn't know what to do with us. The government wouldn't have made the changes to law Torres Strait Islanders wanted themselves. Uncle Steve knew how to talk to people in Brisbane in the department's head office as well as other public servants. Uncle Steve was behind this all the way – he was a leader and an Elder – he showed good leadership and we respected him.

Ivy is now the leader after Uncle Steve passed away. She has a social work background and the cultural integrity focus has changed a bit. It has been hard to replace Uncle Steve.

Now that the legislation has been passed, the Working Party needs to continue down the same road. The commissioner needs an understanding of the full history over the last thirty years. People have to ensure that the information the commissioner has is correct. The history has to be told about there being no positive government response for many years.

The commissioner needs to make sure that the practice is maintained in a cultural way and not the white way. The step of choosing the commissioner is to make sure the practice is maintained the cultural way and not the white way. Customary adoption is practiced differently on Murray Island compared to the Western Islands. If the commissioner is young and legally trained, the person will need to be educated by the Working Party.

The Working Party are needed to ensure and maintain the cultural practice all the way through. There is no point getting someone born on the mainland who hasn't been home and doesn't know the practice. This book should be a history for the people as well as a resource for the commissioner. Steve and Rose have provided the spiritual guidance.

You have my support – I said it publicly at a meeting with the department in Brisbane. You and the former Chief Justice of the Family Court have been the backbone of this struggle.

White resource people need to listen to what Torres Strait Island people say and put it into the jargon government will understand. We need your professionalism and ability to translate what we want to say. White experts have added to the cause, and we appreciate what you have said. You can write English language in a way the government can understand.

I am a social worker, like you and Ivy. Social workers are meant to listen to what people are saying and to get the resources they are asking for. They should listen, hear the message and send the message by translating it into the English language. All that is required is basic social work practice skills.

DANA OBER

The need to legally recognise customary adoption is a common issue in the Torres Strait Islander community. A lot of us are involved in our work and have encountered problems. I was working in a job looking at back payment wages for World War Two veterans and their families. I was on an eligibility review committee considering the claims of the beneficiaries of the veterans who had died, with a lot of the beneficiaries being customarily adopted children. The committee were aware of the issues and lack of documentation. In the 1980s I was the secretariat for the committee and had to research government records.

Customary adoption exists throughout my own family on Saibai Island. I am a cousin to Rose through her dad. Rose told me that a group was forming to look at these issues. At that stage it was not called the Working Party. I became interested in being part of the group. Steve spoke about the issue at national Torres Strait Islander meetings in the 1990s and he invited me to join the group.

I have stayed with the Working Party for thirty years because of the strong leadership from Steve. He really wanted something to be done and we knew we had to stick together to get somewhere.

Working with white resource people was very helpful, as they provided useful information. They either had worked in relevant government departments or at the Family Court and could help us make a stronger case. I believe we should work with people who can help us. Whenever we get help, it makes us more successful. We welcome people who have the expertise and knowledge that we don't have.

Even though we had experienced white resource people, Torres Strait Islanders were always in control of the campaign. The resource people were there to help and to provide their knowledge and expertise.

I didn't have any problems working with them and considered the focus to be putting something to government with professional input.

The retired chief judge was a very important member with legal knowledge from being a judge in that area. I am grateful for his work. The government listened to him because of his status.

It has been very important to have strong leadership throughout this struggle. Steve was very strong and encouraged both committee members and the community to get behind the issue. He is a passionate man.

When Ivy took over leadership from Steve, it was good to have females in charge along with McRose. They both have adopted children as well as being mothers. In addition, they were able to work well with the last group of key politicians, who were all women. That relationship might have been different if Steve was still the leader.

I see the future of the Working Party is to help the commissioner implement the legislation properly. We need to make sure the community is happy about it and let the government know if there are any problems. We need to stick with the issue to bring about social change. When we started the campaign thirty years ago, it was in a hostile political environment. The Labor Party appeared to be interested in the 1990s, but nothing happened. We stayed together until the current Labor Party Government became interested again and this time saw it through.

Steve was passionate about Indigenous rights, and we can't let him down. Although this didn't seem like a controversial issue in the beginning, it took thirty years to achieve legal recognition.

TOMISINA AHWANG (MAM)

Customary adoption has always been recognised as a traditional practice and some community people have thought that we don't need government recognition because we've always had the practice. However, I think it is important to have legal recognition.

I worked for the Department of Social Security in the early 1990s and was aware that families were having issues with their birth certificates. The topic was taboo, and we didn't talk about it. I have seen heartaches when the department has sent letters to the child in their birth name and not their adopted name. ABSTUDY required proof of identity through birth certificates and were telling children that those who they thought were their parents weren't really their parents.

Within our family, there was the matter of Aka (Aunty) Rizah losing her grandchildren. Children have found out about their adopted status through overhearing conversations. We had the problem of being told our practice could only be recognised if it satisfied the western legal system. However, the western system doesn't align with our cultural practice. Finally, we have that recognition after thirty years in the making.

The origins of the Working Party started at the old IINA office in Stanley Street, Woolloongabba, in the 1980s. We were already talking about what to do with the issue when you came on the scene. Your arrival was a godsend for Dad (Steve Mam); it was perfect timing. I have been a part of the long journey to legal recognition because of Dad and his determination to see something achieved. He kept going because of his promise to Aka Rizah.

I feel that I've always been a part of the Working Party. Dad would keep me in the loop, and I would write things for him, even though I lived away for periods of time. I would talk to Dad and Mum every day. I wanted to have a higher profile with the Working Party when Dad died but I wasn't in a good space at the time. I was grieving for Dad and supporting Mum. Dad knew he could trust me and told me that I have a strong will to be able to stand up to government.

The campaign for legal recognition has always been led by Torres Strait Islanders under Dad's leadership. You had a long relationship with us because of the role you played in working with us. In other projects where I have worked with non-Indigenous people, they always try and dictate the game on how things are going to be. We can work with non-Indigenous people if they are genuine and stick around, like you and Alastair. Other people just come and go. Rolf was a good person when he was in government and when he left. He had a genuine commitment to us and was valuable.

Dad is a good judge of character regarding the people he had around him. Mum and I were the first people he would talk to. Uncle Belza has always been suspicious of white people wanting to help and once almost came to fisticuffs with a journalist who was Dad's right-hand man. Dad and I would sometimes clash because we both have strong opinions. When Dad makes a brother, he makes a brother. You, Rolf, and Michael were his main confidants and he treated you three and Alastair as brothers. Overall, you were his main confidant and Dad had 110% trust and confidence in you.

I get frustrated with the political scene in the Torres Strait. It's like I've stepped back thirty to forty years. Mainland Torres Strait Islanders and Aboriginal people are on a totally different thinking level and don't let personalities get in front of the issue. Aboriginal people are so deadly in their political workings, and we've got a lot to learn from them. We have too much pride in the Torres Strait, and it gets in the way.

We have people in our own community that we can't trust because they have another agenda. So, we know who is genuine in government and those who are just doing their job. We could see the people who had a commitment because of their principles, even when they stepped out of their official positions. When Alastair came on board, his presence gave the Working Party extra status.

Torres Strait Islanders are guiding the white resource people, who are the instruments. We have the knowledge, and you have the key that opens doors for our knowledge. We're the knowledge keepers. You interpret for us because you speak the language the government picks up. It's not frustrating to us that government doesn't listen to us because we have you people as partners. We have the traditional knowledge, culture and practice. One can't do it without the other. We have a strong belief that God brought you people to us.

Your relationship with Dad was totally different to his relationship with Alastair. You were with Dad from day one. You were Uncle Paul and Dad had to go to Melbourne and see you after you had your cancer treatment. Dad told me he had to see you because you're his brother. You fit in with his siblings and that doesn't happen overnight. You have to earn it. Dad talked to you all the time on the phone, and you were the reason why we had big phone bills! I have inherited from Dad how he used to tell a long story of background and history before getting to the point.

Legal recognition of traditional adoption happened because of the right timing in the political arena. The legalisation of gay rights, including adoption, before us was an insult to the Working Party who had been trying to achieve legal recognition for many years.

We had strong women working for us in the end, with the legal recognition being led by women. Cynthia Lui was the first Torres Strait Islander member of parliament, also being the Member for Cook, which covers Cape York and the Torres Strait. Shannon Fentiman, Government Champion for the Torres Strait, has always been a strong advocate for women's rights and women's issues. She's another person who is genuinely committed. The premier is also a woman and made a commitment to legalise traditional adoption before the last election.

The Working Party needs to guide the process now that the legislation is in place, and we have a commissioner. We are a resource for government and will ensure that things stay on track. Dad would have allowed government to run over him. The Working Party's job has just begun, and we must make sure the public servants and others don't run away with it.

Ron Castan QC, Eddie Mabo and Professor Garth Nettheim at the first National Torres Strait Islander Conference, Brisbane, 1991. Ron Castan was the barrister who appeared before courts for ten years regarding the Mabo land claim. Eddie Mabo was raised by the Mabo family under the traditional child rearing practice that is the subject of this book. Garth Nettheim was a legal academic best known for his work advancing Aboriginal and Torres Strait Islander rights.

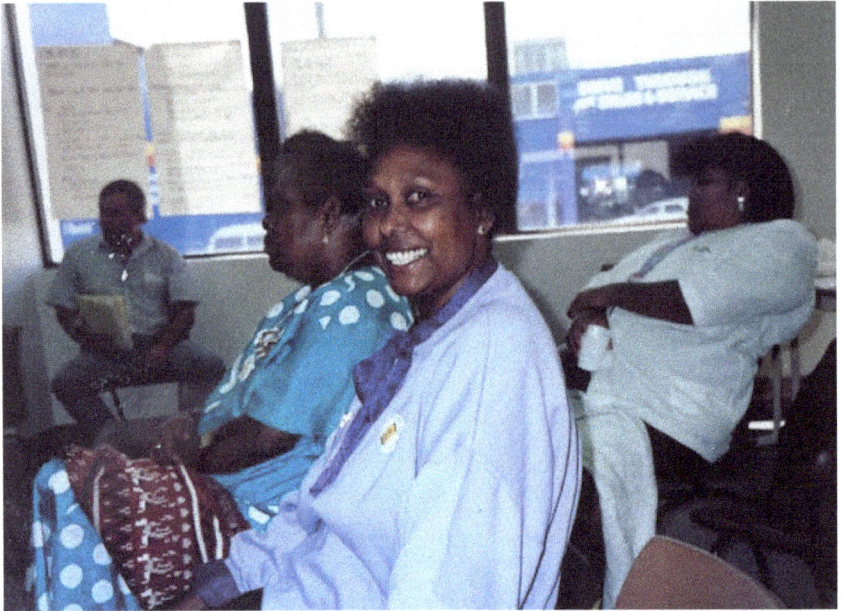

Ivy Trevallion at the first National Torres Strait Islander Conference, Brisbane, 1991.

McRose Elu and Dana Ober at the first National Torres Strait Islander Conference, Brisbane, 1991.

FEATURES

Independence after Mabo

Torres Strait Islanders calling for self-government have found history is on their side, writes KATE COLE-ADAMS.

Robert Tickner (left) on Thursday afternoon with George Mye, an ATSIC Commissioner for the Strait.

December 1992.

Working Party members in discussion before a Family Court conference, Sydney, 1994.

Steve Mam enjoying himself after a National Torres Strait Islander Conference, Brisbane, mid-1990s.

CULTURE

TRADITION

DANALGAU PUI
(KALA LAGAW YA)

THE TREE OF LIFE

IDID IRA LU
(MIRIAM MIR)

HERITAGE

The palm tree is a metaphor for Torres Strait Islander family life.

TORRES STRAIT TOTEMS

Family Court Chief Justice Alastair Nicholson (centre) with Francis Tapim (left) and Steve Mam (right). Children on Mer Island (below).

First there was Mabo. Now a chi justice is seeking Islanders' counsel reforms to anothe controversial legal area. By JOHN LARKIN.

"You people of this island actually set about the most important decision in the High Court *[si]nce the Federation of Australia. It had to be right, and it [w]as right. I'm proud to be standing here in this hall where [it] all started. You showed great courage to take the action, [an]d you led the way for all of Australia."*

[h]igh praise, indeed, for the people of [M]urray Island, and it came from one of [th]e highest law authorities in the land, the [C]hief Justice of the Family Court of [A]ustralia, Alastair Nicholson.

Chief Justice Nicholson had travelled [fr]om Melbourne to Torres Strait, at the [ti]p of Australia, to meet with the island [pe]ople, learn about local family law, see [w]here the Family Court might be able to [as]sist them, and return home with an [un]derstanding which could lead to new [la]w, a better way to work with these orig[in]al Australians, when and if they [re]quired it.

Never before has there been anything [li]ke the head of a federal jurisdiction [si]ing and sitting with Torres Strait [pe]ople under trees and in small halls [su]ch as this one, and telling them he [re]spected their traditions and the integri[ty] of their culture, and wanted people in

his court to understand that as well. It was revolutionary, though in keeping with his reformist nature, and marked a new step in the coming together of white and indigenous people in Australia.

The hall on Murray where the Mabo case was part heard before it ended in the High Court in Canberra in 1992 is a simple room, from which came the genesis of a decision that is not only shaking the whole country, but being used as a model for native title elsewhere in the world.

The meeting place was built of Besser brick, had a concrete floor, handpainted landscape scenes on a back wall, while

through the louvres could be seen the ocean outside. It was at the back of the Murray council chamber, which had a sign outside: "Gelar Meta Ged Sikerarmem" – "This is the law house, where all law and order proceeds."

Torres Strait people have remarkable power. It comes from their having been so self-reliant, with each of the 18 inhabited islands among the hundreds in the region having been kingdoms in their own right, with their own laws, customs and traditions. The people have always been deeply religious and, with the arrival of the missionaries in 1871, known as The Coming of the Light, absorbed Christianity into their own teachings. They have had strict tribal codes of structure, morality and behaviour.

In a way, their being so remote has helped maintain them. The dusty track by the sea through the village on Murray seemed a very long way from the halls of justice in the big cities on the mainland, though Mabo, and now this visit by Alastair Nicholson, were bringing them that much closer.

How close that could or should be remains to be seen. Certainly the Chief Justice and his party took pains to emphasise they were not there to change people. ▷

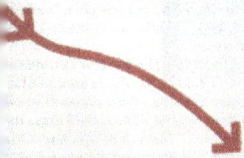

MEET
MAINLAND
FAMILY LAW

What is less definable than the Mabo case is what will be
effect of the Family Court visit, how the two processes of
might find commonality. There were some evident issues, such
the traditional Islander practice of adoption, which is comm
among blood lines as part of the extended family system, and h
that might be affected by white law. Torres Strait Island peop
view life in long-term effect. The Mabo case lasted 10 years.

About 3,000 islanders live in Torres Strait itself, while abc
30,000 are on the mainland, where people were taken in the
days as a source of labour. They are mostly in Cairi
Townsville and Mackay, but also as far south as Sydney
Melbourne and as far west as Perth. They are perhaps me
vulnerable to the effects of the breakdown of tradition
extended families and disputes arising out of mixed marriag

Many white Australians today mistakenly identify Mabo
having begun with the Aboriginal people. The Torres Str
people are aware of the confusion, but are very proud of wh
they did, as they are of being their own people, distinct fr

People travel vast distances to court in open canoes.

the Aborigines, with their own history, culture and custo

At the meeting on Murray (or Mer, to give it its correct tr
being part of three islands which make up the Murray Gro
the Chief Justice said of Mabo: "It made people look at the
and wonder what Australia was like before 1788, when
Aboriginal people and you people were here. Wh
Australians now think about that.

"It started other things to happen. The Federal Governm
says it is going to change the Family Law. As a result of Ma
I said to the Federal Attorney-General: 'What about this M
decision?' " The Chief Justice said that when a child came fr
Torres Strait, the law should take Mabo into account. "A
Mabo, people in my court said: 'What about the people of
land and the people of the sea? Do we know enough ab
them?' I said we didn't, and set up the committee."

He was referring to his establishment in 1993 of a Fan
Court Aboriginal Awareness Committee, headed by Jus
Colleen Moore of Sydney, which seeks to identify indigen
people's special needs, with an emphasis on counselling
mediation. There have already been many Family Court m
ings with Aboriginal groups, as well.

The Chief Justice's visit to Torres Strait developed from
process, from Islanders and court people attending each oth
national conferences over the past couple of years, and fr
the express invitation to go north issued by one of many To
Strait Islanders working for their people on the mainland. T
was Steve Mam, the program and planning consultant v
IINA Torres Strait Islanders Corporation Research and Reso
Centre in Brisbane, a lobbyist with strong political resou
who works in everything to do with Torres Strait people, inc
ing their health, family life, housing, employment and educa

HE FIRST Family Court encounter was
th the chiefs of Torres Strait at an
lander Co-ordinating Council meeting
Thursday Island, at the local bowls
b with its bitumen-like green and views
the sea.

TI, as it is called, has not changed much
the 25 years since I was there. Nobody
rries much, the pandanas and hibiscus
ay in the sea breezes, visitors come
ross by ferry from Horn Island where
e planes land. But there are more shops
w in the main street, along with a new
dio station and a new motel.

The old Grand Hotel burned down a
uple of years ago, leaving a space filled
th memories. TI gets in your blood
ster than a cold beer, and stays there a
longer.

Torres Strait is used to tradition and
bal structure, so the island chiefs had no
fficulty relating to the Chief Justice.
hat would be harder to gauge was what
fect it would have on them to see him
king an initiative and coming to visit
em to see what future course might be
propriate for the Family Court and
lander law.

Despite its isolation, Torres Strait is
aving to face changes which are not as
elcome as we were. It is already evident
the effect on family
'e of white people's
ws. So, though the
uncil elders met the
hief Justice with
spect, there was
so caution.

There were more
an a dozen leaders
ere from the differ-
at islands, still very
uch chieftalins des-
te the Western dress.
he meeting began
th a hymn, a strong-
melodic song with
e sounds of the
uth Seas in the
ices. Then followed
prayer, to invoke
iderstanding. This
uld be common practice over the next
e days. Conversation was conducted in
mixture of Creole, English, broken
nglish and Islander.

Chief Justice Nicholson was concerned,
were the islanders themselves, about
ditional Torres Strait adoption fitting
o a law not really based on concepts of
at sort. It was the main issue raised at
e many meetings over the five days.

"One of the things that I've been urging
the Federal Attorney-General is that
e Family Law Act should be amended,
pecially to require the Court to take
to account the custody of children, law
d custom of the indigenous people of
ustralia, including these islands.

"One of the areas I've detected as a
oblem is the distance to the islands

from Cairns, and the cost involved for
people who need the assistance of the
Court. I'm trying to make arrangements
to reduce the costs."

Joe Cauchi, a director of counselling
with the Family Court, said: "We've come
to learn about your customs and the way
to make decisions
regarding your fami-
lies. We've been
trained in the Wes-
tern way, and it's
important to put our
books aside and
learn about the val-
ues, customs and tra-
ditions. Also, for
many years, Western
traditions have been
imposed on other
cultures. There is a
lot we can learn and
apply to our own
problems. We have
not a good history of
dealing with them."

George Mye, the
chairman from Erub
Island, a most forceful speaker, raised
an example of changes caused by the
white laws. "We used to smack our children, and all of a sudden people came
and said it was cruel and hardship. We
are blaming that outside influence to
spoil our kids today. They are running
wild. It's customary to teach our kids
manners and respect for our elders.
They used to bow to them and now you
don't see that anymore."

Henry Garnier, the ICC chairman,
from Hammond Island, said: "We've
always tried to discipline our children.
Now we're being accused of child abuse.
We have a very high percentage of juvenile crime in the Torres Strait now, and
there's been a backlash. It's getting out of
hand. The only way to control it is to go

back to customary practices. It really
needs to be defined – what is discipline,
and what is child abuse."

Garnier also said that outside influence
had meant single parent benefits were
coming through to mothers in Torres
Strait now, and parents who had previously
given out their children for adoption were
returning to claim them.

Chief Justice Nicholson responded that
the Family Court was concerned with the
issues of child abuse, and sometimes the
difference between that and discipline
was difficult to determine.

George Mye said: "It's in the language.
There are so many ways to say something.
Since the beginning of time there's a difference in doing things. Each island in the
Torres Strait is an entity in its own right,
before the white man. We traded independently, defended our islands – they
fought with Captain Bligh. That's why if
you look at the islands, we have customs
that are respected by Torres Strait as a
whole. There are islands, clans and families, all with different ways.

"We don't want to be white men, blue
men, green men, yellow men. We want to
be Torres Strait Islanders. And to do this,
we have to look at the law of this country
to leave us still as Torres Strait Islanders,
and to be good citizens of Australia."

At the same time, the ICC is planning
native title claims in Torres Strait, of all
the islands, not just the inhabited ones.
They have their own flag.

George Mye: "After 10 years of fighting the Mabo case, we are now having a
respite and pulling our resources together,
and appreciate what the Aboriginal
brothers are doing. It's a common cause.

"We are proud of it [the Mabo case],
and we kept reminding the Queensland ▷

The Age Good Weekend Magazine, May 1995. (pages 40–41)

and Federal governments that this is the only part of Australia that is bordering on a foreign country. We give them our word that if any invasion is going to come to this country – in all likelihood it'll come from the north – and we give everyone our assurance that they'll walk over our dead bodies."

Concern was expressed during our visit about the possible future intentions of Indonesia in the region.

Mye remembered as a boy of 15 watching the dogfights with Japanese aircraft over Thursday Island and seeing the airstrip, on nearby Horn Island, being bombed. He complained that the Islander people were deserted when the evacuation occurred. "They were left like the cats."

Mayor Stephen of the Torres Shire Council at his meeting with the Family Court confirmed that there was a "thinning out of family respect". He said: "Previously your uncle, or another relative, was the law, more than the policeman." In the old days, he said, local custom was not a sensitive issue. Self-consciousness

had come only when people moved off their islands and went to the mainland.

Chief Justice Nicholson has many personal memories of nearby New Guinea, which on Saibai Island we could see just across the water. His parents lived there on a rubber and copra plantation. He said they had had a strong affinity with the local population, among whom he had many friends as a child. "My family also had a close relationship with a remarkable

couple, from the London Missionary Society."

The Holy Trinity church on Saibai, dedicated in 1938 after taking 18 years to build using crushed coral, was the second on the site. The first was erected in 1881 with the coming of the Missionary Society, which had a wide influence in the South Seas. Drums replaced the usual Western church musical instruments and the green wooden doors along the sides rattled in the wind.

In the old meeting hall by the beach, with its louvres and concrete floor, there was again concern that the white welfare system had caused disputes over custody in Torres Strait, with people now wanting to take their children back. This caused other complications, because in the old days it was taboo for children to know they had been adopted.

A speaker insisted that his people were able to work things out in their own way, as a small community of 300. The people plant and harvest by the moon and the sun, and fish and steer their boats by the stars, with remarkable accuracy. Island ▷

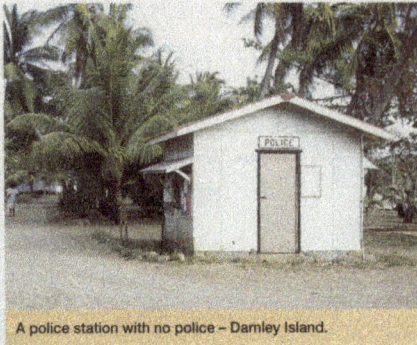
A police station with no police – Darnley Island.

The Women's Voice

THE MURA Kosker Sorority Office on Thursday Island, established in 1988, is dedicated to working towards uniting women of all ages in Torres Strait and the Northern Peninsula Area. It seeks to meet the social, emotional, housing, educational, economic, health, cultural, spiritual and welfare needs of women and their children and dependents. It has a picture of Eddie Mabo on its wall. His widow lives in Townsville.

Their meeting with Chief Justice Nicholson was the first time family violence in the region had been raised during the visit. According to its chairperson, Ellie Gaffney, 100 children were involved in domestic violence in Torres Strait last year, which for a population of 3,000 is a high figure.

All over Australia, we hear that legal services do not represent women, and that those subject to domestic violence do not have fair access to legal services. On Thursday Island the women complained that only two solicitors were provided from the mainland, for two days during court sessions, and were allowed to represent both parties in the relevant cases.

One of the older women at the meeting was Flo Kennedy, known by the common courtesy title of "Auntie". She is credited with having initiated the Mabo case at the beginning of

Ellie Gaffney has a hug for Steve Mam.

the 1980s, but did not proceed as one of the plaintiffs because she was a woman. She said she had chosen Murray Island for the case because the people there had "proved they could stay until the end". She was referring to a 1937 strike when Torres Strait Islanders staged a strike against the Queensland government running their affairs. Torres Strait was annexed in the early 1870s.

As well, said Auntie Flo, the land under claim on Murray Island was distinctly marked and the people there knew their traditions very clearly. "We should have no fear of making decisions about our children if we teach them the customary ways," she said.

Jennie Cooke, a regional director of Family Court counselling, said later: "I was very glad today to have that meeting with the women and hear the issues that concerned them: the care of children, the maintenance of the culture, and also their honesty in confronting the fact that violence is a problem, as it is elsewhere. We heard a strong women's voice at the meeting, and that was very good."

As the meeting ended, Auntie Flo referred to the setting up of the Family Court, with its counsellors and emphasis on people resolving their difficulties, as a unique philosophy in the legal system. Of its coming to Torres Strait, she said: "You will be the first court who understands." □

JOHN LARKIN

The Age Good Weekend Magazine, May 1995. (page 43)

people talk of telepathy. They also told us they related to various totems involving animals. People died showing the signs of their totem, such as shark, turtle or crocodile, acting out the creatures' behaviour. Indeed, when they started showing those symptoms it was understood that they would soon pass away.

The old stories were related by the chief on Mer, Father Gaidam Gisu, who is also the local Anglican priest, as we sat beneath a full moon. He talked about the ancient gods and the coming of the missionaries and of many events in the island's mythology. It confirmed an overwhelming impression that Torres Strait is a universe in itself, and that the islands are spiritual centres, much the same as Aboriginal places, with Mer clearly the centre of the universe and perhaps as important as Uluru is to the Aboriginal people.

On Erub Island, our next stop after Saibai, Chief Justice Nicholson explained: "The Family Court has a tradition of talk, like the traditional way in Torres Strait."

Jennie Cooke, another director of Family Court counselling, who has done a lot of work with Aborigines, said: "It's important if people from Torres Strait ever end up in our court, to understand customs. Also, it's very important because you are Australians. In the past, courts have probably not taken a lot of notice of Aborigines and Torres Strait Islanders."

We heard incredible stories on our trip

People plant and harvest by the moon and the sun, and fish and steer their boats by the stars, with remarkable accuracy. Island people talk of telepathy and relate to animal totems.

of people travelling vast distances in open tin canoes from the outer islands to Thursday Island for the Magistrate's Court sittings. They measured their distance in terms of the number of drums of fuel they needed. Often people preferred to try to settle their differences on their own island. In the case of women involved in family violence cases, they presumably had little hope of getting access to a boat.

From above, Mer, which is right at the start of the Great Barrier Reef, is shaped like a dugong, with the head part reputed to be the place of legends and secret ceremonies. The island is surrounded by huge

fish traps. It has deep water on the village side which is shark-infested, while whales abound in the distance. The island itself is covered in rainforest. The people live on sites once occupied by their ancestors. We were met at the airport by James Rice, one of the plaintiffs in the Mabo case, who argued that the land had been in their families for at least seven generations and had not been, as the Queensland Government argued, empty of ownership before the whites came – the contentious principle of terra nullius.

One of the men at the meeting asked whether in mixed marriages a child would be sent to a home. The Chief Justice said: "The only interest of the court is the best interest of the child, which in the case of Islanders could include looking at grandparents, and also aunts and uncles."

The same man said: "In our society, a single man may adopt a child, and if it's a son, he'll inherit the land."

This is the basis of their argument that the Mabo case in fact has already verified traditional adoption, because that was what happened to Eddie Mabo.

Steve Mam, on behalf of the local people, again asked the question about the differences in law of fostering, guardianship and adoption. "What's the best if I can't bring the kid up any longer?"

Joe Cauchi: "Adoption in the traditional society is done within the same blood line; in the West it is away from the blood line." ▷

"I'm adopted. Eddie Mabo was legally adopted. There's nothing wrong with it. It's just love. When a person goes away and is adopted, he can claim the land. It's in the blood line. It's all across Torres Strait."

Mam: "That's the white man's law?"
Cauchi: "Yes."
Mam: "It sounds as though you got some sorting out to do, as well."

Father Gisu, in one of the most moving speeches heard on the trip, then stood up and declared that the Murray Islands were one vast network. "I'm adopted. Eddie Mabo was legally adopted. There's nothing wrong with it. It's just love. When a person goes away and is adopted, he can claim the land. It's in the blood line. It's all across Torres Strait, all the way to Saibai." His deep voice boomed through the small hall. "When we come to a technical white law, it's called 'legal adoption', but it's in our blood."

Jennie Cooke, commenting on the trip: "It's struck me how the Torres Strait has a culture that's still very strong, and still intact systems of operation, power, authority, social functions and family life, and how little white Australians know about this, how little I knew before I came here.

"It is sad that Australians living in the cities don't know enough about these people who have pride in being Australians. There is all the talk about multiculturalism and the acknowledgement of people coming here, but we don't give the same acknowledgement to the Torres Strait."

Joe Cauchi: "The trip has also been successful in highlighting for the Chief Justice some of the difficulties that they experience through the practice of traditional adoption, the difficulties that arise when an oral culture steeped in history meets another one which places such a high emphasis on documentary evidence to support decisions that are made about families and children.

"If you listen carefully to indigenous people, they don't talk much about therapy and change. They talk about the healing that occurs of the whole person and their environment. There's a deeply spiritual component that permeates their understanding of what people are."

Steve Mam: 'I hope this will be a start to the recognition of customary practices.'

Steve Mam: "This trip is of vital importance. It caters for some of the answers that people have been seeking and need ... not indirectly, but straight from the horse's mouth. And also the Chief Justice is able to listen and understand people better, first-hand. We made him aware."

Asked what his people would do now, he said: "We don't come, and leave it there. I'll do my best to make sure something comes of it. It's only the beginning. I hope it is a start of the work that needs to be done leading up to the recognition of customary practices. In the best world, I'd like to see people get their full rights, and be able to determine their own destiny." ▷

Chief Justice Nicholson said that since joining the Family Court in 1988 he had been concerned that it serviced the cities reasonably well, but did not make much impact outside them, except on the circuit.

"Most of the time I was fighting budgetary difficulties, to keep the Court afloat, rather than engage in extensions. About two years ago, largely through a financial crisis and the very welcome intervention of the then attorney-general, Michael Duffy, I received sufficient funds to put the Court in a position where I was able to start looking at areas we hadn't properly serviced. This included Aboriginal and Torres Strait Islander areas.

"Coincidentally, we were able to start a gender awareness program, funded by the Commonwealth, and I went to Canada, where people in the courts were made more aware of indigenous programs as a spin-off from gender programs. The question asked was: 'If you are being stereotyped in your approach to women' – and I believe that the courts have been – 'then you should examine your attitudes to other areas, such as race and ethnicity.' I said we should use similar methods here to try and overcome these problems.

"Some of the early contacts we made were disturbing. Aborigines who were married to whites felt the system was so white-oriented that they may as well give up and let the other party have the child. We became very aware that there was a fear of courts, which extended to and included ours."

Of the trip itself, "It's opened my eyes to a group of Australians, and a part of Australia, that is entirely different from anywhere else I've seen in this country. I've been impressed by the great physical beauty of the surroundings, and the strength and character of the Islanders. Also, I'm concerned that, being so remote, they and their problems tend to be forgotten, or submerged, in general considerations about Aboriginal issues.

"I also have a feeling that much more could be achieved by a sensitive administration of this area, preferably much more locally oriented than it now is.

"In the area of family, my concerns are that there's insufficient protection of people subject to violence, and inaccessibility to the courts, both Federal and State, to the people of the area. This is not a criticism of the Queensland court system or those who work in it, but rather a criticism of the attitude of government to the staffing and funding of courts.

"I will be sending Justice Colleen Moore, head of the Aboriginal Awareness Committee, along with the director of counselling for the northern region, to Torres Strait to further the discussions that I've had here, with a view to establishing a visiting counselling service to the Torres Strait." He would like to employ Aboriginal and Torres Strait family consultants.

"So far as court sittings are concerned, I will give instructions that where there are disputes in the Torres Strait, judges will be made available to sit as and when required."

The Chief Justice typically wasted no time back on the mainland before describing the situation as urgent. He called on the Federal and State governments to clarify the legal position of traditional adoptions, to avoid continuing confusion and uncertainty. He said he was concerned that rights most Australians took for granted were by way of their inaccessibility denied to many Torres Strait Islanders in remote areas. He believed the Family Law Act should be amended to contain specific recognition of Aboriginal and Torres Strait Islander law and culture and has made a submission to the Attorney-General accordingly.

"In particular, I consider the criteria for determining the best interests of the child, where indigenous children are concerned, should include reference to their traditional law and culture. This would be in accord with the spirit of the High Court's Mabo decision and with the rejection of terra nullius." □

John Larkin is an Adelaide-based writer.

The Age Good Weekend Magazine, May 1995. (page 51)

Pam and Steve Mam with their daughter Darlene, at the National Torres Strait Islander Conference, Brisbane, mid-1990s.

Tomisina Ah Wang (Mam), Ivy Trevallion and McRose Elu at the National Torres Strait Islander Conference, Townsville, 1997.

Bill Lowah, Steve Mam and Tomisina Ah Wang at the National Torres Strait Islander Conference, Townsville, 1997.

Islanders seeking adoption legality

By FRANCINE PULLMAN

FAILURE to recognise Torres Strait Islander customary adoptions could have resulted in the Sambo Agreement rather than the historic Mabo Agreement.

And authorities attending a three-day workshop in Townsville about legalising islander customary adoption, this week remain puzzled about why Eddie Mabo's customary adoptive name, Mabo, was recognised by the government in preference to his birth name, Sambo.

"It would have been very unfortunate if it had been called the Sambo Agreement," said Melbourne social worker and islander expert Paul Ban.

Mr Ban said the ongoing issue of customary adoptions was a sensitive one that was difficult for whites to fully appreciate.

He said Torres Strait Islanders had been campaigning for the past 10 years to have the traditional practice of bloodline adoptions legally recognised.

Unlike immigrant groups who chose to be part of Australia's laws and culture, Mr Ban said indigenous people had white laws thrust upon them.

These did not "gel" with their customs.

"It's not just about birth certificates and social security benefits," he said.

Mr Ban said traditional adoption was an essential part of islander culture which strengthened community and family ties. He said negotiations represented a real chance for whites to give something back to indigenous people.

"And the best thing is it won't cost whites anything (to legalise customary adoption)," he said.

More than 120 islanders and a handful of caucasian government and administrative representatives gathered to thrash out the issue of adoption at a workshop conducted by local community group Magani Malu Kes.

The aim of the meeting was to formulate a strategy for gaining legal recognition of the adoption practices.

Islanders went into a number of discussion groups to try to determine the direction they should collectively take but talks fell into periodic disarray as passions flared.

Parents face family trauma

By FRANCINE PULLMAN

TORRES Strait Islanders Nako and Dana Namok are a colourful couple. Bright floral cloth, traditional jewellery and a lively attitude make them memorable but the issue of illegal customary adoption saddens them.

The Namoks' eldest son, who they declined to name, may not inherit what is rightfully his if negotiations between Torres Strait Islanders and government officials fail.

Like every other Torres Strait Islander gathered at a three-day workshop in Townsville, Mr and Mrs Namok have many adoptive family members.

It is an ancient islander custom practised to strengthen family and community ties and provide children for childless couples.

Mr Namok said traditional adoption was important for heritage reasons, especially if the adopted child was the family's eldest son.

But the wrong name on a birth certificate could cause an adopted child to miss out on his inheritance.

While talks are under way between Islanders and government officials to legalise the adoptions, Mr Namok said he feared his son, now 13, would accidentally discover he was adopted before laws changed.

Because the adoptions remain illegal, many Islander children make the discovery when they first need a birth certificate for school sports, driving licence or passport applications.

FIGHTING RED TAPE . . . Nako and Dana Namok   Photo: MICHAEL CHAMBERS

Mr Namok said it was a traumatic experience for everyone concerned because parents often could not choose their own timing.

"We'll be having a family conference soon," he said.

Townsville Bulletin, April 1997.

Members of the Working Party on Thursday Island, 1999.

The Working Party with Michael Limerick at Thursday Island, 1999.

Torres Strait Islander society's unique system of traditional adoption allows children to be given away within an extended family. The system has been under threat but, as SHELLEY THOMAS reports, the State Government is considering calls to legalise the practice, ending years of suffering

Gifts from

THERE are no world-weary street kids in the Torres Strait. No loveless victims of a spreading urban malaise — just free-spirited "piccaninnies", as the Islander children are affectionately known, live a fitting term for the sea of tiny faces, bare feet and toothy smiles.

"They are gifts from God," explains one mother, watching a group of youngsters play with abandon in the sand, their laughter honest and infectious. Somewhere, a boy pushes a two-wheeled shopping trolley full of trinkets and rust, while others play tag, dangle fishing lines or bomb-dive off a wooden jetty.

Even the sun drags its feet as the day comes to an end, the air thick with the smell of roasted turtle, salt and seaweed. Life moves at the right pace — island-style.

To a stranger, this place is paradise, far from the din and decorum of big city life. The locals, however, know better, although they rarely talk of the dark cloud that has come to haunt their idyll, threatening the very heart of their culture.

Ever since the Queensland Government introduced legislation in the late 1970s, deeming a unique custom of Islander adoption illegal, many families have been torn apart, with the worst case scenario already reflected in a suicide.

The problem, according to Getano Lui (jnr), considered to be the most influential Island leader this decade, is the wrongful imposition of a different culture and a different set

of laws on Torres Strait Islander society — something he claims has contributed to a rise in juvenile crime, alcohol abuse and family breakdown.

Under traditional adoption known as Kupai Werem (which translates to "umbilical cord" and "children"), Islander children are given away within the extended family.

Stemming from a verbal agreement between two families, the transfer of a child can occur to: maintain a family bloodline; strengthen alliances between families; give infertile parents the gift of children;

replace a child who has been adopted out to another family; or provide company and care for an older relative.

"Children are gifts ... they are not our possessions," repeats the mother, wishing to remain anonymous to protect the identity of her own adopted children, one a gift from her sister.

"We don't own our children. Instead, people select who they want to raise their child — it's a great honour."

In the same breath she says Kupai Werem is also the reason Islander women do not contemplate abortion, as infertile couples never face the anguish

of being left childless or elderly people the heartache of spending their last years alone.

"If I'm an infertile woman and I adopt a child, it's not a question of whether you adopt or not, the child is given to you. It's a gift, it's given to you when the woman finds out she's conceived, even before the sex of the child is known."

It is a system Father Scotty Bob, a priest with the Church of the Torres Strait, likens to a truly Christian way of living. Every child is important and each one a blessing.

Moving away from the

Sunday crowd that has gathered outside St Joseph's church on Warraber Island to discuss the normally taboo topic, he says his life would be lacking without Kupai Werem. Like many couples Fr Bob and his wife Sabina were unable to have a family of their own, but were given three children and now have 10 grandchildren.

"Both of us, we got no kids of our own," he says. "We got three adopted children. First one, girl, adopted from my wife's sister and second one, same, we adopted from cousin of my wife. So two of them girls and the boy one from the same sister, my wife's sister.

"It (Kupai Werem) is very important for us but people don't talk about it because if you adopt a kid, you love it and you don't want him to go away."

Ministering to a church "full of plenty piccaninny", Fr Bob is sad that one piece of paper — a birth certificate — is all that stands in the way of a peaceful custom. It's a custom that dates back centuries and still occurs in 95% of families, despite its outlaw status.

Although Kupai Werem has never been legally recognised, birth certificates with adoptive names were "rubber stamped"

by the Queensland Government until the late 1970s when the then Department of Children's Services labelled it illegal under the provisions of the Adoption of Children Act 1964.

The provisions, however, are incompatible with Torres Strait Islander culture, dictating that adoptive parents be selected from a list of candidates who are assessed by departmental officers and unknown to the family.

Above all, the legislation provides no safeguards for parents to wait until 'the right time" to tell children about their adoption — normally

when they are adults — given the fact that birth certificates are required when a child attends secondary school, and later for marriage certificates, driving licences, bank accounts or passports.

Here, the chances of a child or adult accidentally discovering a different surname on a birth certificate are very real, mirrored in the case of a young Thursday Island man who committed suicide after learning the truth while applying for a marriage licence.

"It's as if he felt caught between the devil and the deep blue sea," says Mr Lui, who together with other Islanders has been lobbying state and federal authorities to officially recognise traditional adoption for more than 10 years.

"When children find out the wrong way, through birth certificates, it really traumatises them. They don't know how to react and most of them won't go back to their parents."

Recalling how government officers came to his home on Yam Island in the late 1970s, rounding people into the village hall and bluntly informing children they were adopted, Mr Lui says there was no prior consultation before the legislation was introduced.

"There were plenty of local public servants at the time who understood our culture, but the decision came from the hierarchy in Brisbane. It was done in a very bad way," he says. "I've always said to politicians, don't sit in Brisbane and Canberra and make decisions on our behalf. You have to come

> Children are gifts . . . they are not our possessions. We don't own our children. Instead, people select who they want to raise their child — it's a great honour

February 1999.

BROADCASTER SPENCER HOWSON

ABOVE: Fr Scotty Bob and his wife Babina . . . 'If you adopt a kid, you love it'

LEFT: Piccaninnies at prayer in St Joseph's Church of the Torres Strait

OPPOSITE PAGE: Children are treasured in the Hammond Island community

Pictures: **TOM O'CONNOR**

God

to the Torres Strait, understand our culture and be part of it.

As Island Co-ordinating Council chairman, and former chairman of the Torres Strait Regional Authority, Mr Lui is happy to say the Beattie Government cannot be accused of lethargy.

Soon after taking up office in August, Aboriginal and Torres Strait Islander Policy Minister Judy Spence set about the task of answering the Torres Strait Islanders' calls for change, with a Cabinet submission expected this year.

The submission will cover in-principal support for the legal recognition of Kupai Werem which, if accepted, will then lead to the question of new legislation involving the three departments of Aboriginal and Torres Strait Islander Policy, Justice, and Families, Youth and Community Care.

Appointing a solicitor to deal solely with Kupai Werem, Ms Spence emphasises the need for "legislation of compassion" to recognise traditional adoption as an integral part of Torres Strait Islander culture. If the draft legislation is approved, she says it will be the first to "come from the people rather than being imposed on them".

"They're really not asking for much. They're asking for the legitimacy of a different name to be put on a birth certificate, and I expect my colleagues in Cabinet will be very sympathetic and understanding of the

need to formalise this arrangement.

"It will be an historic event," agrees Mr Lui, referring to Kupai Werem as a key to future peace for his people and their culture.

He is not alone in his belief that legal recognition of Kupai Werem could set an international precedent, particularly in the lead up to the 2000 Olympics, with all eyes focused on Australia.

Well aware of the importance of the proposed legislation, departmental solicitor Susan Jacobs expects the people of Hawaii, Samoa and the Cook Islands to be watching very closely, all having similar adoption practices.

MS JACOBS says the major concern for families under the current legislation is a lack of security in the event of disputes over inheritance or custody.

As she explains, a mechanism is needed to resolve disputes between natural and traditionally adopted siblings over estates without wills, given the fact that Torres Strait Islander people rarely make wills and the majority die intestate.

Likewise, the traditional adoption process is also at permanent risk of being challenged via the Family Court, with biological parents currently maintaining the right to seek custody.

Ms Jacobs says new legislation could also set a standard for other state and territory governments, as well as the

Commonwealth – an opinion shared by Chief Justice of the Family Court of Australia, Alastair Nicholson.

Supporting the legal recognition of Kupai Werem, Justice Nicholson refers to Queensland's proposed legislation as "a good start" to rectifying a problem that needs to be dealt with at a national level.

After visiting the Torres Strait in 1994, he says it is of concern that the custom, which he considers to be part of the Islanders' spirituality, has not been taken into account by any previous government.

Looking ahead, Ms Spence says key issues to be addressed include the question of whether new legislation can be retrospective.

Furthermore, she says a registry of adoption must be central to any legislation to overcome the chance of traditionally adopted children marrying kin in ignorance of their natural relationship, even though there is no evidence of this being a problem at present.

Here, Justice Nicholson advises that such problems should not become a reason for complacency. It is his belief that a process of consultation will produce solutions to all anticipated legal hurdles, with the reasons in favour of change far outweighing those against.

At the end of the day, one reason stands above the rest.

It's there in the trusting face of every child and the hopes of every parent.

ABC Radio breakfast host Spencer Howson has a 25-minute joke up his sleeve just in case the wheels fall off.

It's in his head for the day when catastrophe hits 4QR and there's nothing left but his ready wit and silver tongue.

It's a shaggy dog story about a man becoming a monk. He's told it about a dozen times at parties. His wife Nikki hates it, which is not surprising as she's had six hours of it.

Spencer Howson says he'd be loath to tell it to me, which is decent of him. There are those of us who rank shaggy dog stories alongside accordion-players, ducks flying up the living-room wall, mime artists and women body-builders as matters to be avoided at all costs.

We are lunching at the Royal Exchange Hotel at Toowong, the local for the denizens of the ABC. There ideas are floated, post mortems conducted, rival shows compared, future programs conceived, careers discussed and, if the truth be known, knives metaphorically plunged between shoulder blades. There's a similar pub in Fleet St known as The Stab in the Back.

Spencer, who's 26 and looks younger, reckons he has been in radio 20 years. Born in Preston, Lancashire, he came to Brisbane with his mother in 1978 after his parents split up. He was seven and that year he was given a Christmas present of a cassette recorder.

"I taped my first recording to send a message to my father. I recall I had a big introduction, with theme music, and I told him the time and weather and all the family news.

"I don't know if that engendered in me the idea of a radio career or whether I had the bug beforehand. Chicken-and-egg situation. Anyway, here I am.

– Where he is happens to be in the 5-7.45am slot on the ABC's 4QR.

He studied journalism at the Queensland University of Technology from 1989 to 1991, worked at Brisbane community station 4RPH in 1992 and in 1993 got a job with the ABC in Rockhampton as producer of a morning current affairs show. He took over as host in 1994 and the following year

switched to an afternoon timeslot.

Then the ABC decided that the program could just as easily be produced in Brisbane and he finished at Rockhampton on Friday, June 16, 1995, and started in Brisbane on the Monday.

At the end of 1996 he took over 4QR's breakfast show and has been doing it since.

It's a combination of local news, music, a bit of talkback on lighter matters and interviews with visiting stars such as Billy Connolly and Ben Elton. Its audience is 40 years and over and Spencer Howson takes it, as a compliment when a listener meets him, notes the youngish demeanour and remarks that he comes across much older on air.

"I don't think people in the audience age group have a problem with my being 26 (27 next month). I'm probably mature beyond my years. For 15 years I was an only child and spent a lot of time socialising with my mum's friends.

The electronic media in Brisbane is an incestuous affair. Because of its limited size and the constant meetings at local events, many journalists, producers and others are married to rivals from other media organisations.

Spencer Howson sleeps with the enemy. His wife Nikki is a producer with Channel 9 news. It means keeping mum about some aspects of their work. Don't want your partner stealing your best ideas.

Then there's the fact that half of Brisbane gets to have breakfast with her husband but she doesn't.

(He's a true romantic. He proposed to her at the top of the Eiffel Tower. Like an English gentleman, he asked her father's permission first, then had an agonising 10 days keeping it a secret from her before they got to Paris.)

He likes the immediacy of radio and expects to be in it a long time, though maybe not as long as the bloke in Hobart who did the ABC breakfast show for 42 years.

He fancies one day doing 30-minute documentaries for radio.

If Armageddon does not occur in the interim, he thinks he may deliver his 25-minute epic on his last day in radio. It's a shaggy dog story about a man becoming a monk . . .

– JOHN HAY

ROYAL EXCHANGE HOTEL: 10 High St, Toowong, phone (07) 3371 2555. Spencer Howson had steak and the trimmings and shared a bottle of Bridgewater Mill chardonnay.

PROFILE
Tony Le
Nguyen's
culture
shock
EXTRA

PHOTOGRAPHY
Capturing
Greek lives
EXTRA 6

THE
AGE
SATURDAY 25 MARCH 2000

HERMIONE LEE
Who's not afraid
of Virginia
Woolf?
BOOKS 7

LON
Cha

TRA

SATURDAY EXTRA

Name rights

In a historic move reminiscent of the recognition of land rights, the Family Court has acknowledged the traditional adoption codes of the Torres Strait islanders.

Words: Peter Ellingsen
Pictures: Neil Newitt

Chief Justice Alastair Nicholson of the Family Court and Francis Tapim, chairman of the National Secretariat Torres Strait Islanders, in front of a mural in Murray Island's Law H

IS Honor is beaming across the rickety table that here — in Australia's most remote courtroom — serves as the bench. "What I'm going to do," he tells 50 people, most of them barefoot, "is hear applications for parenting orders." It is a historic moment — the first time the Family Court has sat in the Torres Strait. But none of those gathered in the grey, breeze-block building on the island of Eddie Mabo sits. They sit motionless, staring straight

in a voice louder than the onset outside. Aker, an islander who knows most of those in the room, says: "Him chief make him order for that piccaninny." Pointing to documents before Chief Justice Alastair Nicholson she says in islander Creole: "That paper speak. No one take that piccaninny away from you. Him judge make order piccaninny have name of adopted family."

The sound of 100 hands clapping. Nicholson has offered the 450 people of Mer, or Murray Island, a gift nearly as

Mabo overturned the fiction of terra nullius, opening the door to land rights. Now the Family Court is recognising the traditional adoption code that touches every one of Australia's 30,500 Torres Strait Islanders. And that opens the door to name rights, a power that can be as potent for identity as links to the land.

It has been a long time coming and, while not the amendment to some adoption legislation that islanders want, Nicholson's move, played out across half the 17 inhabited islands of Torres Strait this

forgotten frontier, he has forced the law to tackle the customs of the country's minority, indigenous population.

Not that this is at all clear watching him switch from shorts and talk of fishing to pressed trousers and the most casual sitting the court has known. "Steamy this morning," the chief justice says over a breakfast of cereal at the start of the day. "Not wearing that bloody wig." But he does don a gown and a jabot, the legal bib, before taking his place in Mer's "Gelar Metai", Law House.

around the hall where the Mabo case part heard, and begins his own foray the history books. He is a long way fr the formality of his Melbourne chamb a fact that seems to please him.

No one is going to say "M'lud" on a handy, nine-square-kilometre outcre the start of the Great Barrier Reef, 200 k metres north-east of Cape York, and a than 3000 kilometres from Melbourne. then Nicholson grew up in PNG, and Mer is about as far north as you can and still be in Australia. He's been he

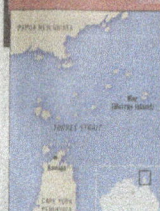

The Age Saturday Extra, March 2000. (cover)

From EXTRA 1

Name

rights

The Age Saturday Extra, March 2000. (pages 4 and 5)

The Working Party meeting in Brisbane, 2005, discussing the delays from the Queensland Government.

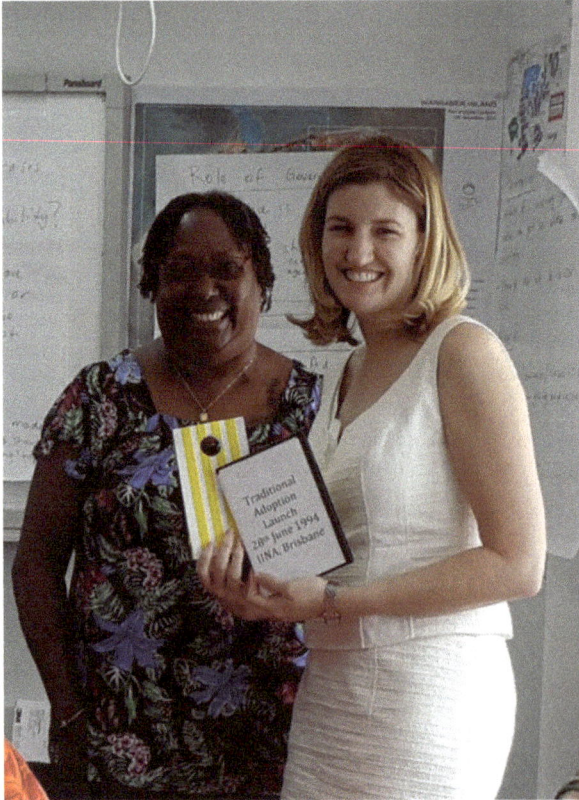

Ivy Trevallion with Shannon Fentiman MP, Cairns, 2016.

Members of the Working Party with Shannon Fentiman MP, Cairns, 2016.

The Honourable Alastair Nicholson meeting with Shannon Fentiman MP in Cairns, 2016, when she first announced the legislation would become a reality.

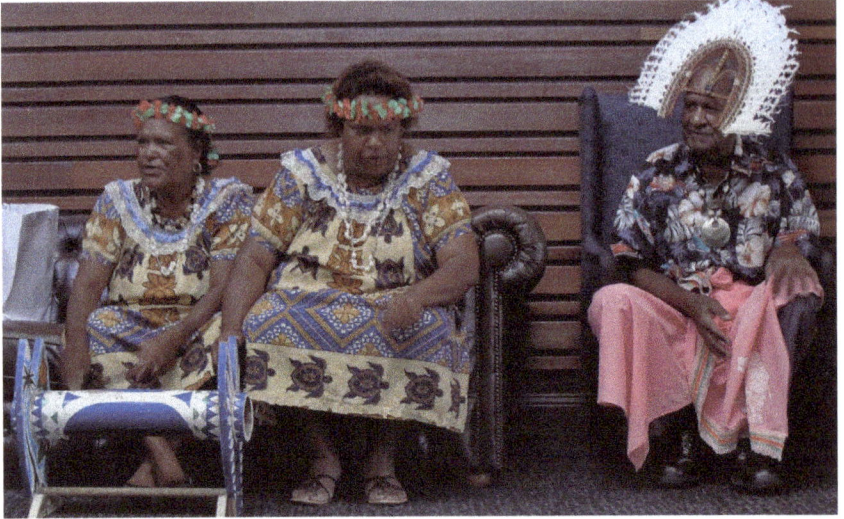

Steve Mam and drummers at Paul Ban's birthday, 2016.

Paul Ban and McRose Elu, Clifton Hill, 2019.

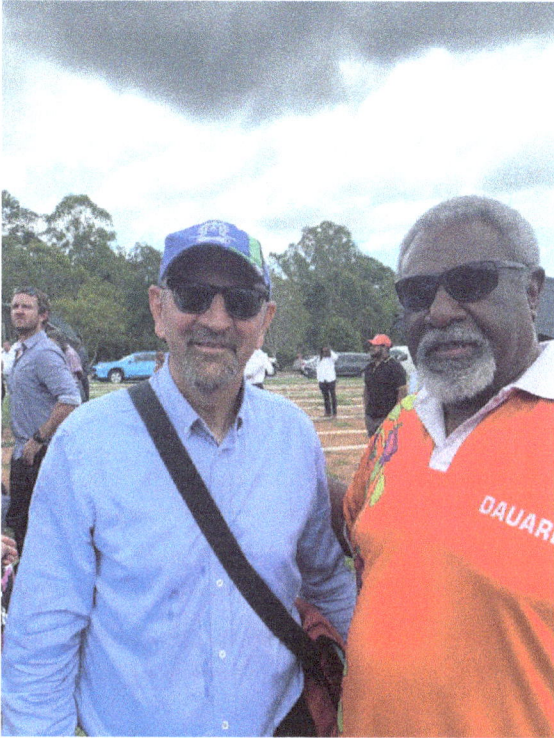

Paul Ban and Charles Passi at funeral of Pam Mam, January 2020.

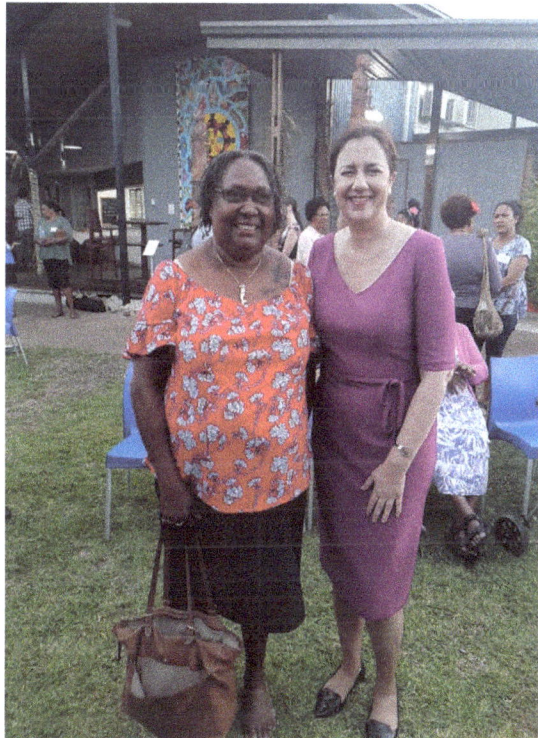

Ivy Trevallion and Premier Annastacia Palaszczuk, Thursday Island, 2021.

Cynthia Lui MP, Member for Cook, Ivy Trevallion, McRose Elu and Shannon Fentiman MP at Parliament House for the passing of the legislation, 1 July 2021.

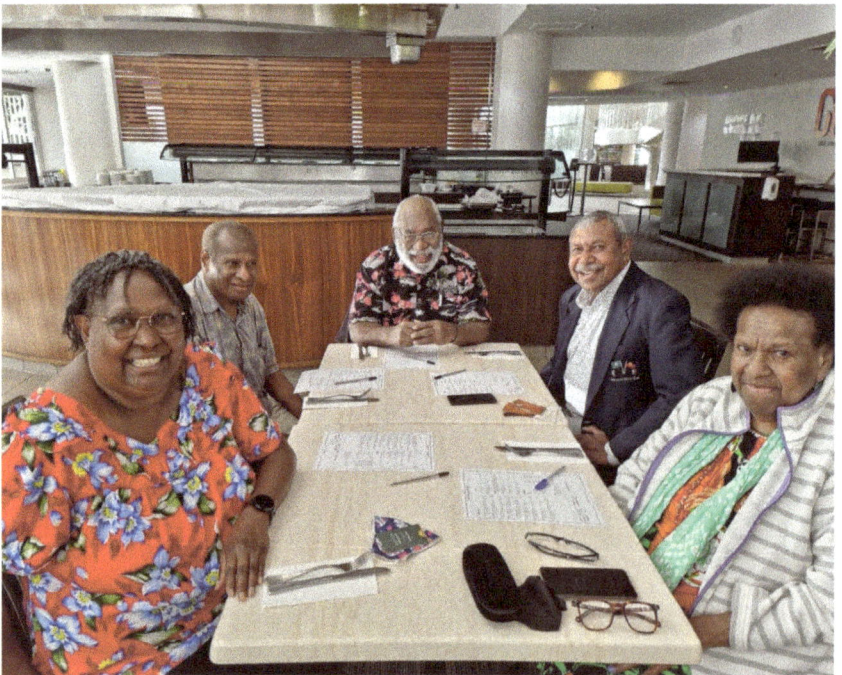

A Working Party meeting, Brisbane, 2021.

Shannon Fentiman MP with Ivy Trevallion and McRose Elu after the passing of the legislation, 1 July 2021.

McRose Elu, Ivy Trevallion and Tomisina Ah Wang at Parliament House for the passing of the legislation, 1 July 2021.

Ivy Trevallion and Michael Limerick at Parliament House for the passing of the legislation, 1 July 2021.

Five members of the Working Party with Charles Passi, Eminent Person, and Craig Crawford MP (both at the back) for the passing of the legislation at Parliament House, 1 July 2021.

Cynthia Lui MP, Member for Cook, Ivy Trevallion, McRose Elu and Shannon Fentiman MP at Parliament House for the passing of the legislation, 1 July, 2021.

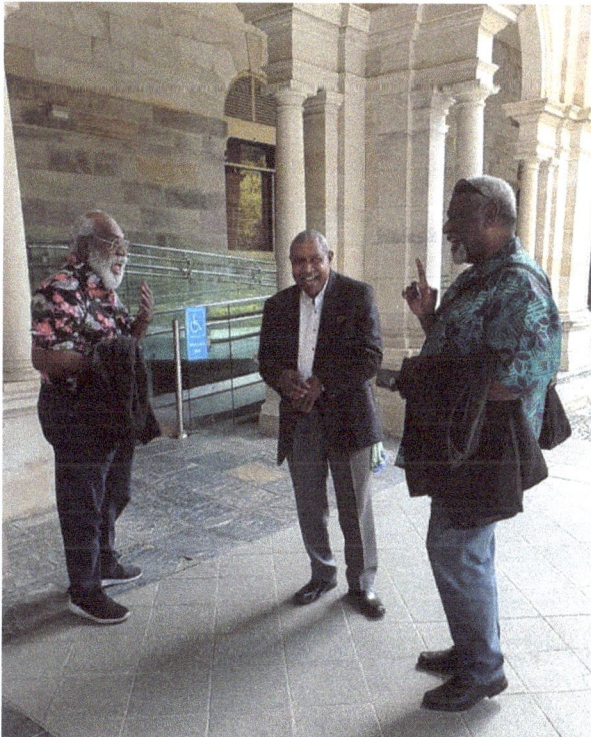

Bill Lowah, Francis Tapim and Charles Passi at the passing of the legislation, Parliament House, 1 July 2021.

Tomisina Ah Wang at the gravesite of her parents, Steve and Pam Mam, 2021.

Paul Ban and McRose Elu, Mornington, Victoria, March 2022.

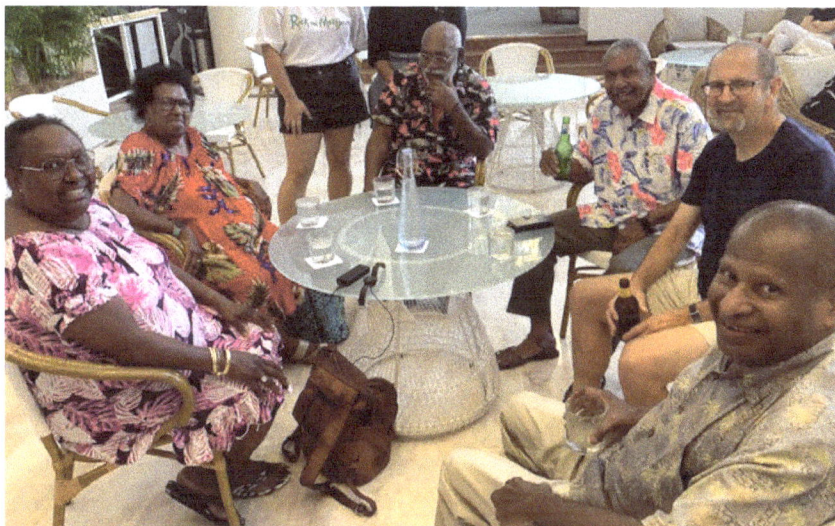

The Working Party relaxing in Cairns, March 2022.

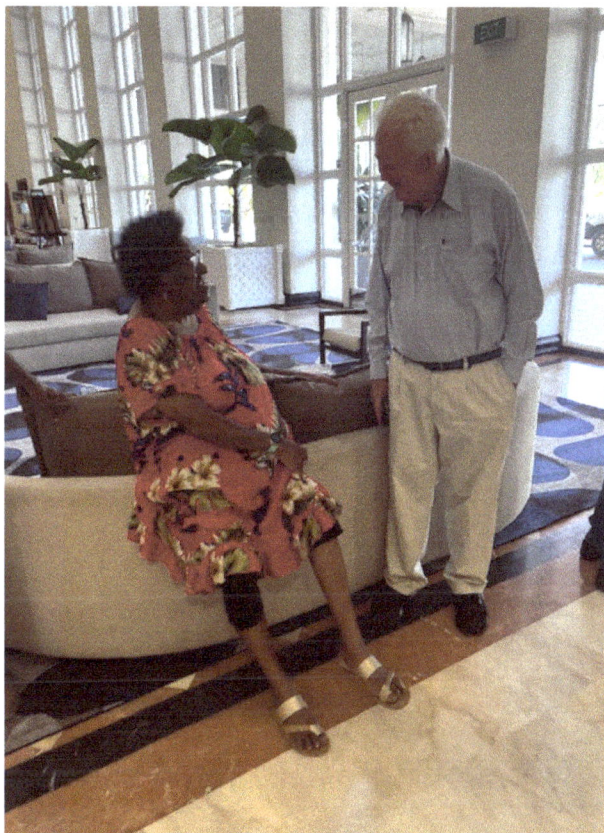

McRose Elu and Alastair Nicholson in Cairns, March 2022.

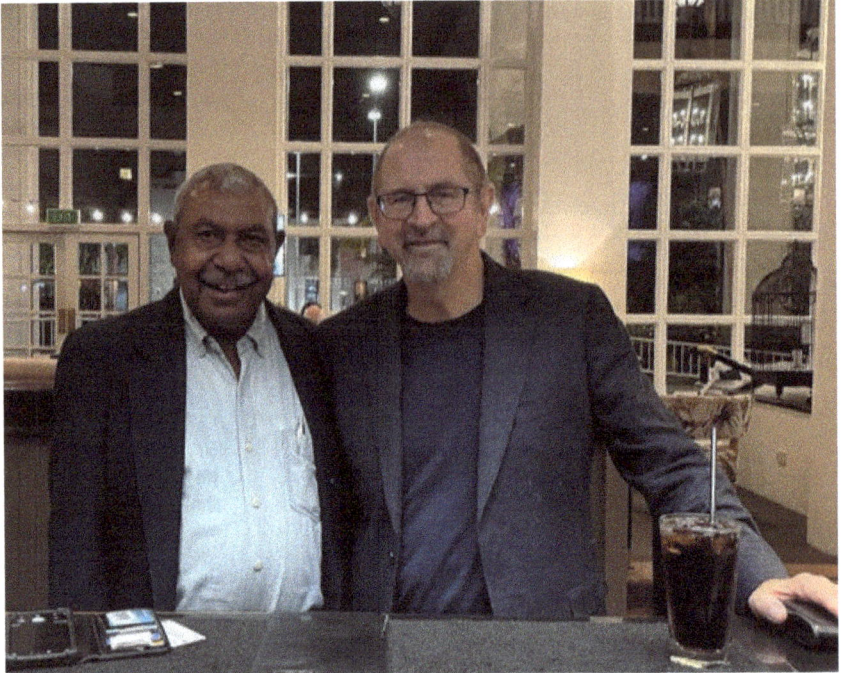

Francis Tapim and Paul Ban, Cairns, June 2022.

THURSDAY 17 MARCH 2022 TORRES NEWS

Group to provide advice on Meriba Omasker Kaziw Kazipa

A formally established advisory group will work to provide advice and guidance to the Queensland Government on the implementation of the *Meriba Omasker Kaziw Kazipa (Torres Strait Islander Traditional Child Rearing Practice) Act 2020*.

Meriba Omasker Kaziw Kazipa Commissioner C'Zarke Maza said the Department of Seniors, Disability Services and Aboriginal & Torres Strait Islander Partnerships (DSDSATSIP – formerly DATSIP) will work in partnership with the advisory group.

"The Meriba Omasker Kaziw Kazipa Advisory Group has been formally established and consists of members of the Kupai Omasker Working Party," Commissioner Maza said.

"The group will play an important role, working to provide advice and guidance on the implementation of the Act.

"Their role is to also ensure DSDSATSIP maintains the cultural

CIRCA 1990-1991: Ivy Trevallion at the 1990-91 National Torres Strait Islander Conference in Brisbane in the formative stages of the Kupai Omasker Working Party, who advocated for legal recognition of Torres Strait traditional child rearing practices. Pic supplied by Paul Ban.

integrity of the application process for legal recognition, while ensuring the application and related processes are confidential, affordable, and accessible to Torres Strait Islander families and communities."

Co-chair Ivy Trevallion said they met with DSDSATSIP for their first meeting in early March at the Pullman Hotel in Cairns.

"The meeting was a success," she said.

"It was also a wonderful opportunity for the members to meet the team from the Office of the Commissioner and the Meriba Omasker Kaziw

Kazipa Program Support Office."

She said members of the new group included the Honourable Alastair Nicholson, McRose Elu, Belza Lowah, Dana Ober, Francis Tapim, Paul Ban and Rolf Nilsson.

Commissioner Maza said the Meriba Omasker Kaziw Kazipa Program Support Offices were now fully staffed in Cairns and Waiben.

"The Program Support Office can also provide information and culturally appropriate support to applicants about the application process," he said.

ADVISORY GROUP MEMBERS: L-R: Belza Lowah, Paul Ban, Francis Tapim & Alastair Nicholson.

LEADING THE WAY: Co-chair Ivy Trevallion & Commissioner C'Zarke Maza. Pics by Aaron Smith.

"All regional DSDSATSIP offices across Queensland can also assist with information."

All enquiries about the application process are welcome and can be made in person, or by email: office@ocmokk.qld.gov.au

or by calling 1800 571 102 (free call) between 9am–4pm Monday to Friday.

More information and relevant forms can also be found at www.ocmokk.qld. gov.au

The Office of the Meriba Omasker Kaziw Kazipa was officially opened 7 September 2021 and Commissioner C'Zarke Maza has since been accepting applications for Cultural Recognition Orders. These applications are independently considered and decided by Commissioner Maza.

The Meriba Omasker Kaziw Kazipa (Torres Strait Islander Traditional Child Rearing Practice) Act 2020 (the Act) was the first of its kind. The Act recognised Torres Strait Islander lore in Western Law and established a process for the legal recognition of Torres Strait Islander traditional child rearing practice.

This ground-breaking Act legally recognised the Ailan Kastom child rearing practice where a child's birth and cultural parents agree, in accordance with Ailan Kastom, that the parental rights and responsibilities for the child are permanently transferred from the child's birth parents to the child's cultural parents.

Torres News, March 2022.

RESOURCE PEOPLE

Interviewed by Paul Ban

ALASTAIR NICHOLSON

I should commence by saying that my experience with Torres Strait Islanders in general has been an entirely positive one, which until now has extended over about thirty years. It has been a great pleasure to be involved with the Working Party over that period and becoming a member upon my retirement as Chief Justice of the Family Court of Australia and a Justice of the Federal Court of Australia in 2004.

There are many points I would like to make regarding why the issue of the legal recognition of Torres Strait Islander child rearing practices has been important to me and well worth pursuing.

The first and the most important was the High Court's legal recognition of customary law in the Mabo case in 1993. It was a catalyst for all other matters regarding legal recognition and customary law. It completely changed the colonial story, by recognising Aboriginal and Torres Strait Islanders as having their own laws and customs which preceded the British law the settlers had imposed upon the country since 1788. Although the legal effect of Mabo has still to be fully worked out, its effect will continue to be felt over many hundreds of years.

The second point is that as soon as I was able, after becoming Chief Justice of the Family Court of Australia in 1988, I wanted to make the Family Court more relevant to Indigenous people.

Many Indigenous people were afraid of the courts and the legal system, often with very good reason. I was examining ways to overcome this concern on their part and to demonstrate to them that the Family Court was a different type of court and in any of its dealing with cases involving children, was bound by law to decide cases in the child's best interests.

I was also examining ways in which I could involve Indigenous people in the processes and management of the court's business so that they, together with judges and court staff, could develop a greater mutual understanding of their problems.

The principle I have always followed when working with other cultural groups, such as Aboriginal and Torres Strait Islanders, is that I am there to assist and not lead. They are not happy about 'wise' people telling them what to do. I can help them by opening doors or suggesting possible viable solutions. When I later worked with Aunty Ivy Trevallion during consultations, it made sense that she should chair the meetings and not me. We whites do not achieve anything by telling people what to do.

This was the background when I was approached by Uncle Steve Mam about a planned Family Court conference in Sydney in 1992. He wanted to make a presentation to the conference on Torres Strait Islander child rearing practices. He spoke of the difficulties Torres Strait Islanders were having with non-recognition of their child rearing practices. I took the view that it would be helpful for judges and staff to see this presentation. It was duly made at the conference and well received. Uncle Steve also asked me to come to the Torres Strait where I could get a greater appreciation of the problem.

I was particularly interested in visiting the Torres Strait. My home had been in Papua New Guinea for most of my childhood, during which I had read extensively about PNG and the Torres Strait. I had always felt affinity for the Indigenous people of both areas and was pleased to be involved with Torres Strait Islanders.

It was at about this time that I also had my first meeting with Paul Ban, who had worked extensively in the Torres Strait. I was aware of his extensive study of Torres Strait child rearing arrangements over many years and he and I have worked closely together since that meeting.

I am conscious that traditional child rearing practices have a spiritual component for Torres Strait Islanders and others such as Uncle Steve spoke about the spiritual aspect. Rose, Belza, Ivy, Tomisina and Dana have been significant people all the way through, along with Francis, who re-joined the Working Party quite recently after a long absence.

I led a small group from the court to the Torres Strait in 1993, not long after the Sydney conference, and we visited various islands, where Uncle Steve addressed the people about the problems arising from the non-recognition of traditional child rearing practices. I continued to be impressed by the magnetism Uncle Steve had and his commitment to this issue and his people and the enthusiasm that they showed for what he was saying. I almost felt I was starting to understand Creole after hearing it spoken at so many meetings.

After hearing of ways in which the court could help, when I returned to Melbourne, we worked on the issue of how the court could make orders to legally secure the transition of a child from one family to another.

We had already decided to appoint Aboriginal and Torres Strait Islander liaison officers to the court's staff, and the late Josephine

Akee was appointed as the first Torres Strait Islander liaison officer based in Cairns. She was later appointed a Member of the Order of Australia for her work. There was also strong support for the proposed program from the then court counsellors based in Cairns, including the director of counselling, Stephen Ralph, who had Aboriginal ancestry and was extremely interested, as were his fellow counsellors.

With their help, and the help of judges, court registrars and other legal staff, and the Working Party, we devised rules of court, designed simple forms, and there was considerable enthusiasm from the people when we visited the islands to explain what we were doing. We tried to develop a workable system that was not too complex.

Josephine Akee went to the islands to explain what we intended and to seek applications for court orders from existing or future receiving parents. Following an application, we needed to be satisfied that the customary arrangement was in the best interests of the child and to this end, Josephine and a court counsellor interviewed the birth and receiving parents and helped them prepare applications to the court.

It was necessary for each of these applications to be heard by a judge and I conducted the first court hearings on the various islands.

In order to demonstrate the involvement and support of the Islanders, judges exercised their powers to appoint two Islanders as assessors to sit with judges hearing these applications. They were usually Elders from each of the islands at which hearings took place. Their function was to assist me in determining that the proper Islander tradition practice had been followed by the parties in each case.

The giving and receiving parents usually gave evidence, together with Josephine Akee and the court counsellor involved. After this, I normally made orders that the child should thereafter live and be in the care of the receiving parents.

Court sittings were thereafter conducted by a number of Family Court judges, and all found the experience worthwhile.

I cannot recall any of these cases that were contested, and this was not surprising because the whole point of making these orders was to give recognition to the traditional cultural practice of child rearing that had already occurred, in some cases years beforehand.

It should be emphasised that these orders differ from the type of orders made under the new Queensland legislation because the Family Court lacked the power to make orders affecting status. This means that birth certificates and passports remained unaltered, and the orders made were not final and could be altered or changed by the court at any time. Importantly, the court could order that the child live with the receiving parents and this was important in the absence of legislation like the new Queensland legislation.

The fact that these orders were made further established the Islanders strong support for a legal solution, and they also established that there were legal solutions to the problems associated with the recognition of the practice and that it was worth pursuing them.

When I returned to the islands for a further consultation in 2018–19, people came up to me and showed me their orders that were made by the court from the late 1990s onwards. Most expressed great satisfaction as to how they had worked out.

However, because of the limitations of Family Court orders, Paul Ban and I, with the support of the Working Party, were anxious to further pursue the issue of new legislation with the Queensland Government to formally recognise the traditional practice.

I had some discussions about the problem with the former Queensland Attorney-General, Ms Linda Lavarch, who had chaired the surrogacy inquiry. She was most helpful and this in turn led to a discussion between Paul Ban and I with the responsible minister at the time, Ms Desley Boyle, who was also the Member for Cairns.

Ms Boyle reacted favourably to the suggestion but said that because of the time that had elapsed, she thought that it would be necessary to hold a further consultation to determine whether views had changed since Paul's earlier consultation.

Further meetings were arranged with her department to discuss the issue and it was eventually decided that a committee of three, of which I would be a member, would conduct a new consultation. The other members were two senior public servants, Shane Bevis, then manager of the Department of Communities, Child Safety and Disability Services, and Carmel Ybarlucea, the director of the Department of Aboriginal and Torres Strait Islander and Multicultural Affairs.

Extensive consultations were conducted over 2011–12 throughout the Torres Strait in each of five island groups, the Northern Peninsular Area and throughout Queensland, which resulted in conclusions remarkably like those reached by Paul Ban in 1993.

The consultations were valuable, however, because they gave a say to many people who had not previously been consulted. The Working Party then made a strong submission to the Queensland Government that legislation should follow to legalise the practice of traditional child rearing in Queensland.

Unfortunately, by this time there had been a change of government in Queensland and the new government displayed little or no interest in taking the matter further.

However, with the election of the first Palaszczuk Government in 2015, there was a change of attitude to this issue and policy development commenced that would eventually lead to legislation being passed in 2021.

From the Working Party's point of view, the meeting that really started the momentum going was a meeting held in Cairns on 16 November 2016.

It was chaired by Aunty Ivy Trevallion and attended by Minister Fentiman, who was then Minister for Communities, Women and Youth, Minister for Child Safety and Minister for the Prevention of Domestic and Family Violence. It was also attended by many senior public servants holding significant and relevant positions in various departments, Paul Ban and myself as advisers to the Working Party, and most of the Working Party itself.

My recollection of the meeting was that it was positive and determined and the first time that I really thought that the proposal was being taken seriously by government and this is borne out by an examination of the agenda.

Although some years were to pass until the legislation was passed, the approach continued to be constructive upon the part of all involved.

There were significant problems in choosing the appropriate legal structure and procedures associated with the new legislation, not least because there were very few precedents to be found for it. This was surprising because the cultural practice is widespread throughout the Pacific, including amongst the Māori people of New Zealand and native Hawaiians.

The only Pacific country that has legislated to approve the practice is Papua New Guinea. It is to be found in the *Adoption of Children Act 1968*. The jurisdiction to make orders lies with the District Court of PNG, under Section 53 of the Act, which deals with adoption by custom. There are some difficulties about the application of these provisions, although my discussions with judges of the Supreme Court of PNG revealed that they saw little difficulty in their application, save that the custom may vary from place to place.

The only other countries in which the practice has gained legal recognition to date are in some provinces of Canada and, to a lesser extent, the USA. We found that the most useful precedent was to be found in the Canadian province of Nunavut, populated by the Inuit peoples. Their practice has significant similarities to that of the Torres Strait Islanders and it has been recognised as part of the law of the province. A major similarity is that the alteration in child raising arrangements takes place first and formal recognition by a state authority takes place subsequently and the legislation allows for access to the courts if the parties are unable to agree.

Something like the practice also occurs in some of the Indian tribes of Canada. In 1993, the British Columbia Court of Appeal held that the parental status of the parents who were members of an Indian Band conferred by custodial adoption was recognised by common law and Section 35 of the *Canadian Constitution Act 1982*. Interestingly the court cited the High Court decision in Mabo in support of its decision, see *Casimel v Insurance Corporation of British Columbia* (1993).

Discussion and policy development continued at the departmental level until in 2018, when the premier announced that the government would legislate to recognise the cultural practice of child rearing.

As part of this announcement, she indicated that a further consultation would be held, to be conducted by three eminent persons, being Aunty Ivy Trevallion, Uncle Charles Passi and myself. Uncle Charles is a well-known Torres Strait Islander from Mer and a son of one of the original Mabo plaintiffs.

This consultation was to be carried out to ascertain the views of the people as to what the legislation should contain. It thus differed from the original consultations, which were as to whether the people thought that the practice should receive legal recognition.

As time was short, we divided the consultations so that most of the consultation in the islands was conducted by Aunty Ivy and me, and most of the mainland consultations were conducted by Uncle Charles, except for major consultations in Brisbane and Cairns, directed at legal, medical and government representatives, and in the Northern Peninsula Area, which were conducted by Aunty Ivy and me.

In Cairns, we received considerable assistance form Judge Josephine Willis of the Federal and Family Court. She was of great help to us in making the court available for consultations with Cairns lawyers, doctors and relevant public servants and participating in those discussions herself. She had considerable knowledge of the issues involved as a result of her practice at the Bar, where she appeared as counsel before me on many occasions in cases that involved Torres Strait Islanders and thereafter as a judge with a particular interest in Indigenous law.

During and following completion of the consultations, work continued at the departmental level over a considerable period. I was able to be involved for much of the early part of this process, but in early 2020, I became seriously ill following a visit that I made to Cambodia, which required frequent hospitalisation over a period of many months. This prevented me from being involved in the important ongoing work in relation to the legislation. Fortunately, Judge Willis was able to take my place in the discussion of these legal issues.

Her assistance did not end there. When the new legislation was presented to parliament, it was referred to a committee and Her

Honour addressed the committee in support of the legislation when it visited Cairns.

By the time that the committee commenced its deliberations in Brisbane, both Paul Ban and I had prepared and lodged papers in support of the new legislation. Unfortunately, because of COVID, we were unable to come to Brisbane to speak in support of it, but we did attend the sittings of the committee by electronic means and were able to answer the committee members' questions and deliver short subsequent written submissions. We were also supported by Professor Helen Rhoades of the University of Melbourne, who had previously chaired the Family Law Council when it delivered a report supporting the legal recognition of the practice.

I think it also important to mention the role of Aunty Ivy in relation to the committee. In addition to making submissions and answering the committee's questions, she accompanied them on their visit to the Torres Strait communities and was able to give them considerable assistance in understanding the issues involved

As is set out previously, the Act was duly passed in 2021.

I had one further involvement in the setting up of the Act's structure and that was to take part in the interviews with the applicants for the position of commissioner under the Act. I had the honour to sit with Kathy Parton, the deputy director of the department and the panel chair, Aunty Ivy Trevallion, for that purpose.

The successful applicant was C'Zarke Maza who has now commenced the challenging task of setting up his office and commencing to put the Act into operation.

He has recruited an excellent staff and is supported by the Working Party at regular meetings that I have had the continued honour of attending.

ROLF NILSSON

My own multicultural background, where English was my second language and I lived in four different countries, helped me appreciate that everyone has a cultural and historical background that works for them. Of most relevance to my work with Torres Strait Islanders was that I lived in Papua New Guinea for a while and could speak pidgin. My experiences growing up meant that I was ripe to see what was going on in different contexts and to accept that people have a right to their own way of expressing who they are.

I first became involved with Torres Strait Islander cultural issues when I was working for the Department of Children's Services, which became the Department of Families in the 1990s. I was writing white papers regarding new child protection legislation and was told to consult with McRose Elu, in the Indigenous Liaison Unit, when I was writing the section on Aboriginal and Torres Strait Islander children. She was in the same government building as me and a couple of floors down. We realised we had a lot in common and that we understood a lot more about each other than we expected.

She raised the issue of customary adoption to me, both through personal experience and culturally, and we had a spiritual connection on the topic through our Anglican and Lutheran backgrounds respectively. I realised there are so many things that are woven together to make a person become part of a family/group/culture. There was a connectivity in discussing Torres Strait Islander adoption and mainstream 'white adoption'. Due to industrialisation, babies were left on the steps of the church to be adopted when the supports in society began to fall apart. However, Torres Strait Islander adoption was not distorted by social disruption and created a loving, sharing, giving maintenance of bonds, ties and connections.

McRose explained that customary adoption used to be 'rubber

stamped' by government and that it was kept separate from white adoption. After it had been stopped with no explanation, she said that Torres Strait Islanders wanted their rights back. I thought that this seemed like a core issue I should be addressing in my role in government.

McRose introduced me to Steve Mam, and I realised that he was a political operative and activist for his people. I connected with him straight away, as he spoke in parables that I could interpret in my language and say back to him, much to his delight. White people used to wonder when Steve was getting to the point. They didn't realise he was making a number of points at the same time. As he spoke, I could see the problems he was raising and was aware that I could access the decision-making processes that contributed to the problem.

I was raised in a family environment where we talked about the mis-interpretation of issues and systems not doing their job because of self-interest and ego. I found that McRose was the heart and soul of the project while Steve maintained the thread of the story. I didn't meet Belza until later and had to cop him giving me a hard time. However, he was satisfied when I gave it back to him. Ivy was also around from the beginning and was supportive of my interest.

I did some homework to find out how it became illegal to rubber-stamp customary adoptions. Fortunately, I had access to documents that weren't secret. It was just that no-one else was interested in them. To my surprise I found out that there wasn't a central policy to make them illegal. Due to regionalisation, bureaucrats in North Queensland adopted a clerical attitude to the process and decided not to process the applications because a report wasn't prepared like in white adoption.

When adoptions became centralised again, Torres Strait Islander adoption had been deemed illegal from the relevant region and this continued to be the position in Brisbane. There was a Canadian social worker in the adoptions section of the department who realised the problem that had been created for the Islanders. She was aware that in Canada there was legal recognition of a similar practice for First Nations people and thought there had been a clerical administrative overkill.

Because I was inside the system, I could support and interpret the conversations between Steve, McRose, Ivy and the bureaucrats. I thought that what happened to the Islanders was a wrong that had to be put right. However, I was told by superiors that even though the problem couldn't be fixed, I was still to share information with the Torres Strait Islanders and show that the government had good intentions, provided I didn't rock the boat.

I thought I had found a simple solution to the problem. If the customary adoption practice was treated as a 'special needs' adoption, as this was the term given to the adoption of all Indigenous children, there was no need for new legislation and there simply needed to be a change in the regulations. However, Anna Bligh, who was the Minister for Families, had made a commitment to her constituents to pass legislation for same-sex adoption before Torres Strait Islander adoption. She didn't want the rights of Torres Strait Islanders to come before the rights of gay and lesbian people. I knew that there was a section of the Department of Families that was promoting the idea of open adoption for white Australians, where birth parents were selecting adoptive parents and thought, 'What's the difference between this and Torres Strait Islander practice?'

I have remained supporting this issue for so long because I hate incompetent public service administration when real people were getting hurt. I treated it as a weaving exercise where I only had one strand and the Working Group were all platting different threads. Although I could add my thread, it was their weaving, their pattern and their cloth.

I saw myself and the white resource people as content experts. The Torres Strait Islanders owned the ship, and we could fix the parts where they didn't have any skills. The culture was leading and those that had integrity with the culture worked with us. We could work with the sharp objects that were tearing at the cloth and could only do small pieces.

The former chief justice, Alastair Nicholson, only led in problem-solving to help otherwise unwilling legal minds to see his interpretation of the issues. He was interpreting the law and I was interpreting administration and politics. You were interpreting the whole context and were the link to get the right white resource people involved.

MICHAEL LIMERICK

I was working in the Department of Aboriginal and Torres Strait Islander Policy Development (DATSIPD) as a young legal officer and was given a special project to work with the Working Party on the legal recognition of traditional adoption. Minister Judy Spence stated it was a priority issue and she had made a commitment to see the matter through to legislation. I read earlier documents on this issue and had worked on Murray Island previously with governance structures. In addition, I was involved with consultation with the Torres Strait Islander community in 1999.

The Department of Families were opposed to legally recognising traditional adoption because they were trying to eliminate grandparent adoptions and didn't want Torres Strait Islanders to have special treatment. I went to a meeting at Parliament House with the Attorney-General, Matt Foley, the Minister for Families, Anna Bligh, and the Minister for Aboriginal and Torres Strait Islander Policy Development, Judy Spence. As they all seemed aligned, I drafted a Cabinet submission and went through the relevant legal issues with the Working Party, especially issues such as ensuring consent of mothers and validating that an adoption arrangement has been genuinely made under Torres Strait custom.

The Cabinet submission was to seek the endorsement of the policy decision before asking for authority to produce the appropriate legislation. We were on Thursday Island engaged in further consultations at a Torres Strait Islander national conference when we heard that Cabinet didn't approve the submission. I was told that the Member for Cook, who was in Cabinet as the Minister for Main Roads and whose electorate covered Cape York and the Torres Strait Islands, did not approve. The reasons were never clear, but I heard it was because he felt there was a risk of more privileged Torres Strait Islanders unduly influencing disadvantaged young mothers to relinquish their babies for adoption.

I felt the moment was lost, as the politicians sided with their factions and my minister rolled over despite earlier publicly claiming her support. My manager in Brisbane told me that the matter was over, I was to be redeployed into another area of work. It was the worst feeling I've ever had as a government officer.

I had formed strong relationships with McRose and Ivy since 1994 and later with Steve and Belza. In addition to the personal connections, I'm a social justice warrior and have done a lot of work on customary law. I thought the Torres Strait Islander issue was a good example to recognise customary law, as there was a clear connection between traditional adoption and white adoption.

A few years later I found myself in a senior position in DATSIPD and had a legally trained Torres Strait Islander working with me. As I had written the framework for the legislation and it was 80% down the road, I thought, 'Let's push it up the flagpole and have a crack.' It was pushed up the hierarchy and met with a deafening silence. I was told, 'If this is an issue for Torres Strait Islanders, why aren't they raising it?' The hierarchy didn't understand that as this was a private and confidential issue with small injustices, Torres Strait Islanders weren't going to go to the media. I realised that this was all about politics.

I always thought this was a good project because it was a practical social issue that wasn't difficult to address. However after realising the lack of will from government at the time indicated it wasn't to go anywhere, it was a salient issue for me in politics and process. After I left the department, I decided not to go to the Bar and completed a PhD in Aboriginal Governance. I worked as a consultant evaluating programs in Aboriginal communities. During that time I maintained my interest in the Torres Strait Islander issue and saw Ivy and McRose off and on.

I came to some Working Party meetings and through the group wrote a submission with Alastair outlining a procedure for legal recognition of customary adoption that could be done safely. I had contact with Julie Conway, who was leading a government inquiry into surrogacy. Although the Torres Strait Islander issue was different, it gave them an opportunity to present their case to government again. My attendance at Working Party meetings was to give legal background information and provide moral support.

My motivation to stay with the issue was that I had committed relationships with the Torres Strait Islanders. There was a principle to uphold and personally I had unfinished business. I was happy to put in my own time and was surprised when my nephew, Shane

Bevis – a public servant in Shannon Fentiman's office – told me the matter was going to be cranked up again. He told me he was going to the Torres Strait with Alastair for consultations. I think this is a wonderful story of persistence and patience.

I had no problem allowing the project to be led by the Torres Strait Islanders, as when I started in 1999 the Working Party had been leading it for at least ten years. When I went through the records, I found they had been pushing the case for change since the late 1980s. I was twenty-eight and saw myself as an enabler with a strong principle to empower and not to lead in governance. My interest was in capacity building and not in telling people what to do.

I have felt guilty that I hadn't put in more time when the issue bubbled up again over the past several years, although I have always seen my role as supporting and not leading. I have always made time to come to meetings and contribute advice and ideas when the Working Party has invited me. I was deeply humbled at the celebration of the passage of the law through parliament last year when Ivy publicly acknowledged the role I had played in helping the Working Party. She said that I had taught them to understand the legislation and the legal issues to be overcome to achieve their goal of legislative recognition. It's been a privilege working with the Working Party – it's like being embraced into a family. I've realised that it has often been easier working with Torres Strait Islander people than Aboriginal people, as Aboriginal people have been treated more unjustly by government and have good reason to be suspicious of white good intentions.

PAUL BAN

My own interest had developed out of my professional background as a family and child welfare social worker. I had worked for a number

89

of years in the field of substitute childcare, where children were placed by social workers into a range of settings when they could no longer live with their parents. These settings included foster care, family group homes, residential care and adoption.

After I had begun my work with Torres Strait Islanders when I was working for the Department of Children's Services in Cairns, from 1982 to 1984, I was impressed by the developments in child welfare in New Zealand during the 1980s. Due to the ratification of the Treaty of Waitangi, their government made constructive responses to the needs and wishes of Māori people. They introduced child welfare legislation that reflected the strength of Māori extended family in resolving childcare matters through holding family group conferences and applied this same approach to work with European and other non-Māori families (*Children, Young Persons, and Their Families Act 1989*).

I attended a conference in Melbourne, the International Conference on Adoption and Permanent Care, in 1988 with a group of Torres Strait Islanders where this development was presented by a group of Māori and non-Māori child welfare workers. I was impressed that a whole country was promoting legislation and practice based on the same topic that the Torres Strait Islanders and I were presenting in a workshop: 'What Can White Australians Learn from the Traditional Adoption Practice of Torres Strait Islanders?'.

The developments in New Zealand and the theme of the workshop presentation were that kinship-based societies can offer white nuclear-family-based society the opportunity to think more laterally about how to manage issues of 'child welfare'. This includes consideration of the relationship between the carers of children and those who are unable to care for them for varying periods of time. It also includes thinking more broadly about the notion of identity and belonging, as well as viewing the concept of 'the best interests of the child' within a societal rather than individual framework.

When I began my work with Torres Strait Islanders in Brisbane at the end of 1986, I had not worked as a social worker for almost two years and enrolled in 1985 to undertake a Master of Social Work research thesis. Consequently, I did not see myself as a social worker at the time. I thought that I was approaching Torres Strait Islanders in Brisbane as an individual who had experience in the Torres Strait (four years with a child welfare department based in Cairns in the 1970s and early 1980s) and who was interested in helping them promote their customary adoption practice to the Queensland Government.

I expected the first key Torres Strait Islander I approached at IINA, a Brisbane-based Torres Strait Islander organisation, to respond positively to my interest. However, I was challenged by Bill Lowah, who has since become a lifelong friend. I was surprised when he told me that white researchers are always wanting to examine Indigenous people and take their findings away with them. He was also concerned about my professional label of 'social worker', as it carried with it historical connotations of the disempowerment of Indigenous families rather than my belief that I wanted to strengthen and learn from Torres Strait Islander family customs.

Alarm bells went off for Bill based on his experiences with both white social workers and white researchers. I have since realised that the social work identity I was trying to minimise was actually a strength that made me a useful resource person to the Torres Strait Islander community. My training had taught me the theory and skills of community work through community development strategies. In addition, I was also trained to work as an advocate in an empowering capacity.

These frameworks allowed me to treat the Torres Strait community as both a community of connectedness through shared experience and through the ties of kinship. I was able to inform and resource them through my capacity to relate with white government departments and professional groups, such as lawyers. In addition, I was able to develop strategies and options for the Islanders so that they could make their own informed choices about how to manage their affairs in this area. I had to ensure that I was not leading the process of decision-making or negotiating with government departments without always checking back with the Torres Strait Islanders who had developed trust in me.

Steve Mam was a community leader and the main person I wanted to see in Brisbane to begin my research. However, Bill Lowah tried to protect Steve Mam from having to deal with me by discouraging me. His words were, 'I'm not going to stop you, but I'm not going to help you.' Consequently, I approached McRose Elu. McRose had studied anthropology at the University of Queensland and showed immediate support for my interest in the legal recognition of customary adoption. As she was a member of IINA and well-connected to Steve Mam, I was introduced into the Brisbane-based Torres Strait Islander community by her and eventually established a link with Steve.

My contact with these two resulted in me becoming a resource person to IINA and undertaking consultancies and attending workshops through funding IINA received from DATSIPD (Queensland Government). It also led to a long history of working and developing a strong friendship with Steve, McRose, Bill and the rest of the Working Party.

McRose later told me that when we first met, she listened to what I was proposing as, 'You did not speak like a white man usually does.' She stated that whereas white people are normally direct and confronting, I spoke 'around' the issue for a while and 'there was something in the tone of your voice when you finished speaking that was genuine.' McRose further stated that her father taught her to listen carefully to what people are saying before responding. In addition, she sensed I was interested in a topic that was of personal interest and relevance to her (she had recently traditionally adopted a child and had adopted children within her family).

Steve Mam stated he has always respected McRose's strong sense of people's character, and initially accepted me both on Rose's recommendation and the fact that he had personal experience of traditional adoption himself. Both Steve and McRose stated they have a strong spiritual belief that I was led by a greater power to come to them. Their spirituality resonated with my own beliefs, and I was drawn to their amalgam of Christianity and 'Islander spirituality' due to my Christian upbringing.

Steve told me that he usually comes across white people who are direct, take information away and are never seen again. Both he and McRose stated they were initially prepared to accept me at face value and watch how I behaved. They commented that I always acted in deference to their leadership and continually checked with them to ensure they were happy with what I was doing. Due to my experience in working with the Department of Children's Services in Cairns for four years, I was strongly aware of the difficulties white people face gaining trust with Black communities.

I observed Indigenous people becoming used to having control taken from them by white authorities under a range of guises, both overt and covert. I was determined to show Steve and McRose that I was genuine and felt their 'testing' me was only to be expected. McRose and Steve stated that their judgement of me was vindicated by the fact that I maintained consistent involvement with them over a long period of time in a private capacity. Steve told me that I was one of only a handful of white people he totally trusts to speak on his behalf, as he knows I will always check back with him before I say anything.

I believe I would have had far greater difficulty obtaining acceptance if I was dealing with Aboriginal communities. Steve said that Aboriginal people have told him that 'Torres Strait Islanders crawl or grovel to the white man, as they are too trusting.' He explained that he and Rose grew up in the Torres Strait and were less used to 'white ways of thinking and operating' than their children, who have grown up in Brisbane. They admitted that they were lucky enough to have strong traditional roots to language and customs. They are secure in their identity as Torres Strait Islanders. He stated that Bill Lowah had grown up with white people and due to his personal experience was always suspicious of their motives.

Torres Strait Islanders have benefited from a less traumatic contact history with whites than Aboriginal people and are able to interact with white individuals and institutions without experiencing the same levels of racism and marginalisation. Their invisibility to whites relates more to their homeland being geographically isolated from white Australians and the fact that they are Melanesian and not considered by white Australians to have the same negative attributes as Aboriginal people.

Steve and McRose told me that they had previous dealings with and knowledge of white people who abused the 'trusting nature' of Torres Strait Islanders, as they misrepresented information they obtained and did not respect taboo or private information. However, they stated they still maintain their trust in people who are genuine.

During an interview I had with McRose and Steve in October

2005 when I saw them in Brisbane, they asked me to organise a meeting the following day with senior staff from DATSIPD to find out why there had been no information given to them about the government's response to the legal recognition of traditional adoption. The meeting took place as requested, with McRose and Steve wanting to know why there had been no feedback for almost six years. We had been told since 1999, along with the other Torres Strait Islanders involved with the project, that the matter was to be referred to the Queensland Law Reform Commission.

However, we were informed at the meeting that DATSIPD could not afford to fund the Law Reform Commission the budget required to undertake the task. As they could not get help from other departments they were 'pursuing other options' but were not prepared to reveal what those were. The public servants further stated that the Queensland Government had greater priorities at the time than recognising customary adoption, and as they had to brief a new minister, they were unsure what action he would take. In response to Steve Mam's request for DATSIPD to fund a community meeting of Torres Strait Islanders in Brisbane to be told the outcome of their six-year wait, the public servants stated they preferred to simply phone him to let him know what the minister had decided.

Their response was dismissive and disempowering. There was no explanation as to why they did not consider informing Torres Strait Islanders at various times over the six years why there had been no progress with the issue.

Steve later commented that he felt the intended referral to the Law Reform Commission was a delaying tactic in any case, as 'everything they have considered to do with Indigenous customs has cobwebs on it.'

The positive developments since that time began when Alastair

Nicholson retired as Chief Justice of the Family Court of Australia in 2004 and began his role as a valuable resource person to the Working Party. There was a seamless merge from him becoming a member of the Working Party and eventually becoming Uncle Alastair, like my identity becoming Uncle Paul. Somewhere along the way Rolf Nilsson, former policy officer with the Department of Children's Services, became Uncle Rolf.

IMPACT OF THE NEW TORRES STRAIT ISLANDER LEGISLATION ON PACIFIC NATIONS

Customary 'adoption' practice is widespread throughout the Pacific region in island nations. The practice exists alongside formal, state-regulated adoption processes. However, in most nations the state does not recognise or accommodate customary adoption, giving rise to a number of practical problems like those faced by Torres Strait Islanders.

Throughout the Pacific, customary adoption occurs within extended families and operates outside formal legal processes. It has occurred for as far back as families can remember and has continued to take place after they were colonised and either the British or French legal systems were imposed on them. Adoption laws were intro-duced under colonial administration and were based on a western understanding of adoption. Customary adoption is not regulated by any formal law. The consequences are like those the Torres Strait Islanders faced in dealing with the Queensland Government. The impact is that 1) there is no process for determining the best interest of the child, and 2) there are no safeguards because of an absence of due process and there is no official confirmation of status. Papua New Guinea is the only Pacific island country that formally recognises customary adoption in its legislation.

The *Meriba Omasker Kaziw Kazipa (Torres Strait Islander Traditional Child Rearing Practice) Act 2020* can be considered a possible model for Pacific countries, as it talks about 'traditional child rearing practice' rather than using the word 'adoption' and talks about law as 'Ailan Kastom', which is an Indigenous language term and avoids confusion with western law.

The impact of the thirty-year struggle of Torres Strait Islanders to finally achieve legislative recognition of a traditional family custom can benefit the same struggles their much larger Pacific neighbours are experiencing.

CONCLUSION

This book is not an anthropological study of Torres Strait Islander and Pacific customary child rearing practices, which anthropologists referred to as 'adoption' practices by referencing western culture. It is not a legal analysis of customary and western law, and it is not a policy document regarding the implementation of the Bill that became an Act of parliament on 1 July 2021.

It is a story of a group of people who stayed together as a support and lobby group for thirty years in order to bring about legal recognition of a family practice that is integral to Australia's Indigenous minority group. Most Australians don't know much about Torres Strait Islanders, let alone that they have a customary child rearing practice that has more similarities to Pacific and Inuit cultures than Aboriginal Australians.

The group of people known as the Working Party, a name that was adopted during the formation stages and has remained, comprise of Torres Strait Islanders and non-Torres Strait Islanders who had no idea it would take thirty years to achieve their goal. Ron Castan QC, the barrister who represented Eddie Mabo and others in the Queensland courts and the High Court of Australia, in 1990 encouraged the group to prepare for the long haul, as it had taken the land rights case ten years before success in the High Court of Australia in 1993.

This book is both a record of the journey as well as reflections of the members, along with other supporters, of the power of Indigenous and non-Indigenous people working together in true partnership.

Due to the historic significance of what has been achieved, the Working Party wanted their journey to be documented and gave me permission to compile this book. They would like it to be a record of an outcome that none thought was likely thirty years ago due to the negative attitudes of the Queensland Government at the time.

There is a likelihood that the long-fought battle for achievement could be overlooked as time passes and the focus changes to ensuring a successful implementation of the legislation.

www.ingramcontent.com/pod-product-compliance
Lightning Source LLC
Chambersburg PA
CBHW041258040426
42334CB00028BA/3078